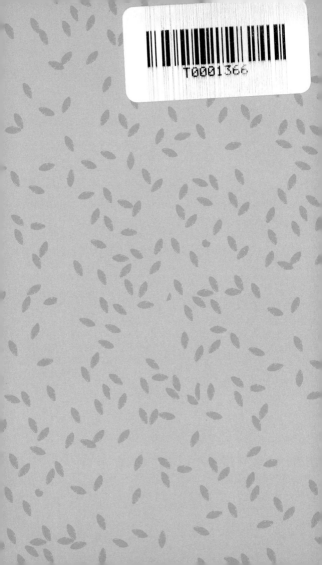

OUR PLACE IN
NATURE

More anthologies available from
Macmillan Collector's Library

No Place Like Home ed. Michèle Mendelssohn

Why Friendship Matters ed. Michèle Mendelssohn

On Your Marks ed. Martin Polley

The Art of Solitude ed. Zachary Seager

Food for Thought ed. Annie Gray

The Joy of Walking ed. Suzy Cripps

OUR PLACE IN NATURE

Selected Writings

Edited and introduced by
ZACHARY SEAGER

MACMILLAN COLLECTOR'S LIBRARY

This collection first published 2022 by Macmillan Collector's Library
an imprint of Pan Macmillan
The Smithson, 6 Briset Street, London ECIM 5NR
EU representative: Macmillan Publishers Ireland Ltd, 1st Floor,
The Liffey Trust Centre, 117–126 Sheriff Street Upper,
Dublin 1, DOI YC43
Associated companies throughout the world
www.panmacmillan.com

ISBN 978-1-5290-7580-9

Selection, introduction and author biographies © Zachary Seager 2022

The Permissions Acknowledgements on p. 213 constitute
an extension of this copyright page.

1 3 5 7 9 8 6 4 2

A CIP catalogue record for this book is available from the British Library.

Cover and endpaper design: Mel Four, Pan Macmillan Art Department
Typeset by Jouve (UK), Milton Keynes
Printed and bound in China by Imago

MIX
Paper | Supporting
responsible forestry
FSC
www.fsc.org
FSC® C116313

Visit www.panmacmillan.com to read more about all our books
and to buy them.

Contents

v

Introduction

ZACHARY SEAGER

At all times and in all places, in wonder, horror or concern, human beings have puzzled over our place in nature. Thunder on the mountain brought fear and awe – had we done wrong? The harvest was plentiful and the seasons were clement – had we done right? Was nature hostile, was nature good? How best were we to live with it, respond to it, respect it?

Every culture throughout history has had a clear conception of nature. In myths and religions around the world there have been mountain journeys and fasts in the desert, river crossings and catastrophic floods, bounded gardens and star-filled skies which have formed the core of our spiritual narratives. Many have imagined, like the Greek poet Hesiod (*c.* 750–650 BCE), a golden age in the deep past marked by harmony with the natural world. Many, like Hesiod, saw this age as irretrievable. Humans, after a fall, had to struggle against nature.

Centuries later, still in classical antiquity, a popular poetic genre took shape, the pastoral, which from Theocritus (*d.* after 260 BCE) to Virgil (*d.* 19 BCE) focused on the rustic life of shepherds. These bucolic poems were tailored to an urban readership who imagined life in the countryside to be simpler and more natural than in Athens or Rome. In the late Middle Ages in Europe, travel accounts by literary-minded voyagers offered fantastical descriptions of exotic creatures, honey-coloured streams, trees gleaming with fruit and strange stunning birds. These extraordinary flora and fauna promised that, elsewhere, humans had a different relationship to their environment.

In the West, something changed in the early modern period. Stimulated by the scientific revolution and a major shift in religious attitudes, many thinkers felt a growing need to provide rational accounts of nature and its processes. This scientific impetus demanded close observation of natural phenomena. From the mating habits of salmon to the divergent forms of different ferns, we studied the world, described it. Humans remained apart, as if alien on our planet, in nature but not of it.

This novel scientific impulse was predicated on an ancient idea, man's dominion over nature. Departing from theological notions of stewardship, scientists and philosophers reconceived the natural world, theorizing it as a system that could be accurately measured and judiciously controlled. René Descartes (1596–1650), for instance – that emblematic innovator at the birth of modern science – argued that scientific methods could render humans 'masters and possessors of Nature'. This renewed vision of the natural world laid the foundations for modernity. It led to the titanic taxonomies of the eighteenth and nineteenth centuries, exhaustive catalogues which separate life into distinct domains, each a kingdom unto itself.

There was some resistance. Romantic writers in the late eighteenth century attacked the inheritors of Descartes's vision. Nature rationalized and tamed was a cold monstrosity. Spiritually corrupt and morally degrading, it destroyed a sublime mystery. Later, through the long intellectual, political and literary traditions which led from Romanticism to modern environmentalism, thinkers around the world deployed new concepts in the fight. Preservation, for instance, which sought to protect natural landscapes, and new forms of conservation, which aimed to better protect natural resources. One or both of these approaches, it was thought, could stave off future ruin. Meanwhile, those blindly viewed as uncivilized – Native Americans, for example, and other Indigenous peoples – looked on with mounting dread.

The ideas of conservation and preservation have had a lasting impact on our relationship to nature. But the temptation to mastery is, for many, irresistible. Taking Descartes at his word, science and industry under capitalism have radically transformed the planet, rendering us at last masters and possessors of our world. This has led to our present moment, which some scientists have termed the Anthropocene. Derived from the Ancient Greek word *anthropos*, human, this is a geological epoch of our very own. Our impact on the environment has been so enormous, it is claimed, that we have utterly transformed the planet to meet our whims. But our well-reasoned actions have had unintended consequences, and we have had to relearn the ancient lesson taught in poetry and religion: the world has whims of its own. As the planet defends itself from human domination, our drive to dominion may lead to our destruction.

Throughout history, then, ideas about our place in nature have shifted and clashed, disappeared and resurfaced, been formulated and reformulated in response to different pressures. These competing conceptions have been captured in literature, most notably in the genre known today as nature writing. An outcrop of the scientific mission to comprehend and master the world, modern nature writing emerged in the eighteenth century. It was pioneered by British country parsons like Gilbert White (1720–93) who, intrigued by natural history, described the fauna and flora he found around Hampshire. Now a diverse and thriving genre, nature writing favours detailed descriptions of striking environments, and scrupulous accounts of animals and plants.

There is a stereotype of the classic nature writer as a gifted stylist absorbed in their study. Rigorously attentive to the natural world and intent on the complexity of its interlocking systems, they leave little room for emotion or for a wider sense of our own place in nature. This might be true of certain scientific texts, but in the masterpieces of nature writing, many of which are included in this anthology, it is rarely the case. Henry David Thoreau (1817–62), for instance, permanently strives through his work to cultivate a stronger bond with the natural world.

But writing about nature isn't necessarily *nature writing*, and many authors in this collection who wrote before or after the codification of the genre cannot be recognized in the term. The Japanese author and court lady Sei Shōnagon (*c.* 966–1017 or 1025), for example. For over a thousand years, Japanese poets have drawn their imagery and metaphors from the changing seasons, helping to frame the right conduct of life. That doesn't make Lady Sei – as she is sometimes known – a nature writer.

The writings in this anthology are not bounded by one category. Although all attend to the natural world with meticulous care, the works, like their authors, are all different in their way. Some – Robert Louis Stevenson (1850–94) or the explorer and travel writer Isabella Bird (1831–1904), for example – see adventure in the wild. Others, like Rachel Carson (1907–64), seek to better understand our world to better protect it.

The authors in this collection have one thing in common. They all raise profound questions about our role on this planet: how we interact with the complexity of the natural world; how we might best respect and appreciate nature; whether we should work to preserve or conserve it, or reshape it as we wish; and what nature can do for our spiritual, emotional and intellectual life. Implicitly or explicitly, they all ask a question posed since humanity emerged: what is our right relation to the natural world?

From thrilling accounts of swifts and praying mantises to lyrical descriptions of survival in the Mojave Desert, from the changing seasons in the

Pacific to silent spring mornings in tenth-century Japan, from an alligator attack in north Florida to reflections on the common toad in London N1, this anthology brings together powerful and emotive writing about our experience with the natural world. Whether outlining the stewardship principles of the Lakota in North America or delighting in the miracles of one's own private garden, every author in this collection is intensely conscious of our place in nature. Some call for spiritual growth through contact with the natural world. Others argue against our work-till-you-collapse ideology, finding a warning and a remedy in the cycles of the environment. Still others call for action, and, in devastating prose, demand that we preserve forests and mountain valleys, and protect the sea and coastal lands. Some, despite all, even find hope.

OUR PLACE IN
NATURE

THE WIDE WORLD

RACHEL CARSON
1907–1964

Born in Springdale, Pennsylvania, near the Allegheny River, Rachel Carson spent much of her career with the United States Fish and Wildlife Service. Employed to cultivate public interest in the bureau's work, she used her spare time to pitch articles on marine life to magazines and newspapers. An essay in the *Atlantic Monthly* earned her a publishing deal and led to her first book, *Under the Sea Wind* (1941). Her second book, *The Sea Around Us* (1951), also focuses on aquatic life. In stunning detail, it describes the sea in all its forms, from the birth of an island to the curves of ocean-floor canyons, from rainfall in the Pacific to the lifecycle of plankton. It won her a National Book Award and financial independence, allowing Carson to devote herself to conservation. Her final work, *Silent Spring* (1962), made her a household name. A thundering account of the destruction wrought on the world by pesticides such as DDT, it became a rallying cry for the environmentalist movement. It led to significant changes in US agricultural policy, if not, as Carson had dreamed, to enduring restraint in our domination of the planet. *The Sea Around Us*, excerpted here, is typical of her writing. Complex and gorgeous, it combines scientific rigour with the highest literary qualities, staging the fluctuations of the ocean as a life-and-death narrative filled with beauty and wonder.

from *The Sea Around Us*

For the sea as a whole, the alternation of day and night, the passage of the seasons, the procession of the years, are lost in its vastness, obliterated in its own changeless eternity. But the surface waters are different. The face of the sea is always changing. Crossed by colors, lights, and moving shadows, sparkling in the sun, mysterious in the twilight, its aspects and its moods vary hour by hour. The surface waters move with the tides, stir to the breath of the winds, and rise and fall to the endless, hurrying forms of the waves. Most of all, they change with the advance of the seasons. Spring moves over the temperate lands of our Northern Hemisphere in a tide of new life, of pushing green shoots and unfolding buds, all its mysteries and meanings symbolized in the northward migration of the birds, the awakening of sluggish amphibian life as the chorus of frogs rises again from the wet lands, the different sound of the wind stirs the young leaves where a month ago it rattled the bare branches. These things we associate with the land, and it is easy to suppose that at sea there could be no such feeling of advancing spring. But the signs are there, and seen with understanding eye, they bring the same magical sense of awakening.

In the sea, as on land, spring is a time for the renewal of life. During the long months of winter in the temperate zones the surface waters have been absorbing the cold. Now the heavy water begins to sink, slipping down and displacing the warmer layers below. Rich stores of minerals have been accumulating on the floor of the continental shelf—some freighted down the rivers from the lands; some derived from sea creatures that have died and whose remains have drifted down to the bottom; some from the shells that once encased a diatom, the streaming protoplasm of a radiolarian, or the transparent tissues of a pteropod. Nothing is wasted in the sea; every particle of material is used over and over again, first by one creature, then by another. And when in spring the waters are deeply stirred, the warm bottom water brings to the surface a rich supply of minerals, ready for use by new forms of life.

[...]

In a sudden awakening, incredible in its swiftness, the simplest plants of the sea begin to multiply. Their increase is of astronomical proportions. The spring sea belongs at first to the diatoms and to all the other microscopic plant life of the plankton. In the fierce intensity of their growth they cover vast areas of ocean with a living blanket of their cells. Mile after mile of water may appear red or brown or green, the whole surface taking on the color of the infinitesimal grains of pigment contained in each of the plant cells.

The plants have undisputed sway in the sea for only a short time. Almost at once their own burst of multiplication is matched by a similar increase in the small animals of the plankton. It is the spawning time of the copepod and the glassworm, the pelagic shrimp and the winged snail. Hungry swarms of these little beasts of the plankton roam through the waters, feeding on the abundant plants and themselves falling prey to larger creatures. Now in the spring the surface waters become a vast nursery. From the hills and valleys of the continent's edge lying far below, and from the scattered shoals and banks, the eggs or young of many of the bottom animals rise to the surface of the sea. Even those which, in their maturity, will sink down to a sedentary life on the bottom, spend the first weeks of life as freely swimming hunters of the plankton. [...]

Under the steady and voracious grazing, the grasslands of the surface are soon depleted. [...]

In the spring the sea is filled with migrating fishes, some of them bound for the mouths of great rivers, which they will ascend to deposit their spawn. Such are the spring-run chinooks coming in from the deep Pacific feeding grounds to breast the rolling flood of the Columbia, the shad moving into the Chesapeake and the Hudson and the Connecticut, the alewives seeking a hundred coastal streams of New England, the salmon feeling their way to the Penobscot and the Kennebec. For months or years these fish have known only the vast spaces of the ocean. Now the spring sea and the maturing of their own bodies lead them back to the rivers of their birth.

Other mysterious comings and goings are linked with the advance of the year. Capelin gather in the deep, cold water of the Barents Sea, their shoals followed and preyed upon by flocks of auks, fulmars, and kittiwakes. Cod approach the banks of Lofoten, and gather off the shores of Ireland. Birds whose winter feeding territory may have encompassed the whole Atlantic or the whole Pacific converge upon some small island, the entire breeding population arriving within the space of a few days. Whales suddenly appear off the slopes of the coastal banks where the swarms of shrimplike krill are spawning, the whales having come from no one knows where, by no one knows what route.

[...]

A hard, brilliant, coruscating phosphorescence often illuminates the summer sea. In waters where the protozoa Noctiluca is abundant it is the chief source of this summer luminescence, causing fishes, squids, or dolphins to fill the water with racing flames and to clothe themselves in a ghostly radiance. Or again the summer sea may glitter with a thousand thousand moving pinpricks of light, like an immense swarm of fireflies moving through a dark wood. Such an effect is produced by a shoal of the brilliantly phosphorescent shrimp Meganyctiphanes, a creature of cold and darkness and of the places where icy water rolls upward from the depths and bubbles with white ripplings at the surface.

[...]

As the fall advances, there are other movements, some in the surface, some hidden in the green depths, that betoken the end of summer. In the fog-covered waters of Bering Sea, down through the treacherous passes between the islands of the Aleutian chain and southward into the open Pacific, the herds of fur seals are moving. Left behind are two small islands, treeless bits of volcanic soil thrust up into the waters of Bering Sea. The islands are silent now, but for the several months of summer they resounded with the roar of

9

millions of seals come ashore to bear and rear their young—all the fur seals of the eastern Pacific crowded into a few square miles of bare rock and crumbling soil. Now once more the seals turn south, to roam down along the sheer underwater cliffs of the continent's edge, where the rocky foundations fall away steeply into the deep sea. Here, in a blackness more absolute than that of arctic winter, the seals will find rich feeding as they swim down to prey on the fishes of this region of darkness.

Autumn comes to the sea with a fresh blaze of phosphorescence, when every wave crest is aflame. Here and there the whole surface may glow with sheets of cold fire, while below schools of fish pour through the water like molten metal. Often the autumnal phosphorescence is caused by a fall flowering of the dinoflagellates, multiplying furiously in a short-lived repetition of their vernal blooming.

[...]

Like the blazing colors of the autumn leaves before they wither and fall, the autumnal phosphorescence betokens the approach of winter. After their brief renewal of life the flagellates and the other minute algae dwindle away to a scattered few; so do the shrimps and the copepods, the glassworms and the comb jellies. The larvae of the bottom fauna have long since completed their development and drifted away to take up whatever existence is their lot. Even the roving fish schools have deserted the surface waters and have migrated into warmer latitudes or have found equivalent warmth in the deep, quiet waters along the edge of the continental shelf. There the torpor of semi-hibernation descends upon them and will possess them during the months of winter.

The surface waters now become the plaything of the winter gales. As the winds build up the giant storm waves and roar along their crests, lashing the water into foam and flying spray, it seems that life must forever have deserted this place.

[...]

But the symbols of hope are not lacking even in the grayness and bleakness of the winter sea. On land we know that the apparent lifelessness of winter is an illusion. Look closely at the bare branches of a tree, on which not the palest gleam of green can be discerned. Yet, spaced along each branch are the leaf buds, all the spring's magic of swelling green concealed and safely preserved under the insulating, overlapping layers. Pick off a piece of the rough bark of the trunk; there you will find hibernating insects. Dig down through the snow into the earth. There are the eggs of next summer's grasshoppers; there are the dormant seeds from which will come the grass, the herb, the oak tree.

So, too, the lifelessness, the hopelessness, the despair of the winter sea are an illusion. Everywhere are the assurances that the cycle has come to the full, containing the means of its own renewal. There is the promise of a new spring in the very iciness of the winter sea, in the chilling of the water, which must, before many weeks, become so heavy that it will plunge downward, precipitating the overturn that is the first act in the drama of spring. There is the promise of new life in the small plantlike things that cling to the rocks of the underlying bottom, the almost formless polyps from which, in spring, a new generation of jellyfish will bud off and rise into the surface waters. There is unconscious purpose in the sluggish forms of the copepods hibernating on the bottom, safe from the surface storms, life sustained in their tiny bodies by the extra store of fat with which they went into this winter sleep.

Already, from the gray shapes of cod that have moved, unseen by man, through the cold sea to their spawning places, the glassy globules of eggs are rising into the surface waters. Even in the harsh world of the winter sea, these eggs will begin the swift divisions by which a granule of protoplasm becomes a living fishlet.

Most of all, perhaps, there is assurance in the fine dust of life that remains in the surface waters, the invisible spores of the diatoms, needing only the touch of warming sun and fertilizing chemicals to repeat the magic of spring.

MARY HUNTER AUSTIN
1868–1934

Poet, essayist, novelist, and playwright, feminist and activist, advocate of Native American and Spanish-American rights, Mary Hunter Austin was celebrated in her lifetime for the range and abundance of her creative output. Born in Carlinville, Illinois, her family relocated to the West Coast in 1888. Among the desert landscapes of California and New Mexico, her writing flourished. She catalogued Native American myths and described the shepherding industry in California, wrote plays and founded theatres, and collaborated with the noted photographer and environmentalist Ansel Adams (1902–84). After her death, Austin's work suffered a period of neglect. Rediscovered in the late twentieth century, her works are now recognized as classics of nature writing. Her book *The Land of Little Rain* (1903), excerpted here, is a stunning tribute to the High Sierra and Mojave Desert, the fauna and flora which survive and thrive there, and the spiritual life the landscape can cultivate.

from *The Land of Little Rain*

East away from the Sierras, south from Panamint and Amargosa, east and south many an uncounted mile, is the Country of Lost Borders.

Ute, Paiute, Mojave, and Shoshone inhabit its frontiers, and as far into the heart of it as a man dare go. Not the law, but the land sets the limit. Desert is the name it wears upon the maps, but the Indian's is the better word. Desert is a loose term to indicate land that supports no man; whether the land can be bitted and broken to that purpose is not proven. Void of life it never is, however dry the air and villainous the soil.

This is the nature of that country. There are hills, rounded, blunt, burned, squeezed up out of chaos, chrome and vermilion painted, aspiring to the snow-line. Between the hills lie high level-looking plains full of intolerable sun glare, or narrow valleys drowned in a blue haze. The hill surface is streaked with ash drift and black, un-weathered lava flows. After rains water accumulates in the hollows of small closed valleys, and, evaporating, leaves hard dry levels of pure desertness that get the local name of dry lakes. Where the mountains are steep and the rains heavy, the pool is never quite dry, but dark and bitter, rimmed about with the efflorescence of alkaline deposits. A thin crust of it lies along the marsh over the vegetating area, which has neither beauty nor freshness. In the broad wastes open to the wind the sand drifts in hummocks about the stubby shrubs, and between them the soil shows saline traces. The sculpture of the hills here is more wind than water work, though the quick storms do sometimes scar them past many a year's redeeming. In all the Western desert edges there are essays in miniature at the famed, terrible Grand Cañon, to which, if you keep on long enough in this country, you will come at last.

Since this is a hill country one expects to find springs, but not to depend upon them; for when found they are often brackish and unwholesome, or maddening, slow dribbles in a thirsty soil. Here you find the hot sink of Death Valley, or high rolling districts where the air has always a tang of frost. Here are the long heavy winds and breathless calms on the tilted mesas where dust devils dance, whirling up into a wide, pale sky. Here you have no rain when all the earth cries for it, or quick downpours called cloud-bursts for violence. A land of lost rivers, with little in it to love; yet a land that once visited must be come back to inevitably. If it were not so there would be little told of it.

This is the country of three seasons. From June on to November it lies hot, still, and unbearable, sick with violent unrelieving storms; then on until April, chill, quiescent, drinking its scant rain and scanter snows; from April to the hot season again, blossoming, radiant, and seductive. These months are only approximate; later or earlier the rain-laden wind may drift up the water gate of the Colorado from the Gulf, and the land sets its seasons by the rain.

The desert floras shame us with their cheerful adaptations to the seasonal limitations. Their whole duty is to flower and fruit, and they do it hardly, or with tropical luxuriance, as the rain admits. It is recorded in the report of the Death Valley expedition that after a year of abundant rains, on the Colorado desert was found a specimen of Amaranthus ten feet high. A year later the same species in the same place matured in the drought at four inches. One hopes the land may breed like qualities in her human offspring, not tritely to "try," but to do. Seldom does the desert herb attain the full stature of the type. Extreme aridity and extreme altitude have the same dwarfing effect, so that we find in the high Sierras and in Death Valley related species in miniature that reach a comely growth in mean temperatures. Very fertile are the desert plants in expedients to prevent evaporation, turning their foliage edgewise toward the sun, growing silky hairs, exuding viscid gum. The wind, which has a long sweep, harries and helps them. It rolls up dunes about the stocky stems, encompassing and protective, and above the dunes, which may be, as with the mesquite, three times as high as a man, the blossoming twigs flourish and bear fruit.

There are many areas in the desert where drinkable water lies within a few feet of the surface, indicated by the mesquite and the bunch grass (*Sporobolus airoides*). It is this nearness of unimagined help that makes the tragedy of desert deaths. It is related that the final breakdown of that hapless party that gave Death Valley its forbidding name occurred in a locality where shallow wells would have saved them. But how were they to know that? Properly equipped it is possible to go safely across that ghastly sink, yet every year it takes its toll of death, and yet men find there sun-dried mummies, of whom no trace or recollection is preserved. To underestimate one's thirst, to pass a given landmark to the right or left, to find a dry spring where one looked for running water—there is no help for any of these things.

Along springs and sunken watercourses one is

surprised to find such water-loving plants as grow widely in moist ground, but the true desert breeds its own kind, each in its particular habitat. The angle of the slope, the frontage of a hill, the structure of the soil determines the plant. South-looking hills are nearly bare, and the lower tree-line higher here by a thousand feet. Cañons running east and west will have one wall naked and one clothed. Around dry lakes and marshes the herbage preserves a set and orderly arrangement. Most species have well-defined areas of growth, the best index the voiceless land can give the traveler of his whereabouts.

If you have any doubt about it, know that the desert begins with the creosote. This immortal shrub spreads down into Death Valley and up to the lower timber-line, odorous and medicinal as you might guess from the name, wandlike, with shining fretted foliage. Its vivid green is grateful to the eye in a wilderness of gray and greenish white shrubs. In the spring it exudes a resinous gum which the Indians of those parts know how to use with pulverized rock for cementing arrow points to shafts. Trust Indians not to miss any virtues of the plant world!

Nothing the desert produces expresses it better than the unhappy growth of the tree yuccas.

Tormented, thin forests of it stalk drearily in the high mesas, particularly in that triangular slip that fans out eastward from the meeting of the Sierras and coastwise hills where the first swings across the southern end of the San Joaquin Valley. The yucca bristles with bayonet-pointed leaves, dull green, growing shaggy with age, tipped with panicles of fetid, greenish bloom. After death, which is slow, the ghostly hollow network of its woody skeleton, with hardly power to rot, makes the moonlight fearful. Before the yucca has come to flower, while yet its bloom is a creamy cone-shaped bud of the size of a small cabbage, full of sugary sap, the Indians twist it deftly out of its fence of daggers and roast it for their own delectation. So it is that in those parts where man inhabits one sees young plants of *Yucca arborensis* infrequently. Other yuccas, cacti, low herbs, a thousand sorts, one finds journeying east from the coastwise hills. There is neither poverty of soil nor species to account for the sparseness of desert growth, but simply that each plant requires more room. So much earth must be preëmpted to extract so much moisture. The real struggle for existence, the real brain of the plant, is underground; above there is room for a rounded perfect growth. In Death Valley, reputed the very core of desolation, are nearly two hundred identified species.

Above the lower tree-line, which is also the snow-line, mapped out abruptly by the sun, one finds spreading growth of piñon, juniper, branched nearly to the ground, lilac and sage, and scattering white pines.

There is no special preponderance of self-fertilized or wind-fertilized plants, but everywhere the demand for and evidence of insect life. Now where there are seeds and insects there will be birds and small mammals, and where these are, will come the slinking, sharp-toothed kind that prey on them. Go as far as you dare in the heart of a lonely land, you cannot go so far that life and death are not before you. Painted lizards slip in and out of rock crevices, and pant on the white hot sands. Birds, hummingbirds even, nest in the cactus scrub; woodpeckers befriend the demoniac yuccas; out of the stark, treeless waste rings the music of the night-singing mockingbird. If it be summer and the sun well down, there will be a burrowing owl to call. Strange, furry, tricksy things dart across the open places, or sit motionless in the conning towers of the creosote. The poet may have "named all the birds without a gun," but not the fairy-footed, ground-inhabiting, furtive, small folk of the rainless regions. They are too many and too swift; how many you would not believe without seeing the footprint tracings in the sand. They are nearly all night workers, finding the days too hot and white. In mid-desert where there are no cattle, there are no birds of carrion, but if you go far in that direction the chances are that you will find yourself shadowed by their tilted wings. Nothing so large as a man can move unspied upon in that country, and they know well how the land deals with strangers. There are hints to be had here of the way in which a land forces new habits on its dwellers. The quick increase of suns at the end of spring sometimes overtakes birds in their nesting and effects a reversal of the ordinary manner of incubation. It becomes necessary to keep eggs cool rather than warm. One hot, stifling spring in the Little Antelope I had occasion to pass and repass frequently the nest of a pair of meadowlarks, located unhappily in the shelter of a very slender weed. I never caught them sitting except near night, but at midday they stood, or drooped above it, half fainting with pitifully parted bills, between their treasure and the sun. Sometimes both of them together with wings spread and half lifted continued a spot of shade in a temperature that constrained me at last in a fellow feeling to spare them a bit of canvas for permanent shelter. There was a fence in that country shutting in a cattle range, and along its fifteen miles of posts one could be sure of finding a bird or two in every strip of shadow; sometimes the sparrow and the hawk, with wings trailed and beaks parted, drooping in the white truce of noon.

If one is inclined to wonder at first how so many dwellers came to be in the loneliest land that ever came out of God's hands, what they do there and why stay, one does not wonder so much after having lived there. None other than this long brown land lays such a hold on the affections. The rainbow hills, the tender bluish mists, the luminous radiance of the spring, have the lotus charm. They trick the sense of time, so that once inhabiting there you always mean to go away without quite realizing that you have not done it. Men who have lived there, miners and cattle-men, will tell you this, not so fluently, but emphatically, cursing the land and going back to it. For one thing there is the divinest, cleanest air to be breathed anywhere in God's world. Some day the world will understand that, and the little oases on the windy tops of hills will harbor for healing its ailing, house-weary broods. There is promise there of great wealth in ores and earths, which is no wealth by reason of being so far removed from water and workable conditions, but men are bewitched by it and tempted to try the impossible.

You should hear Salty Williams tell how he used to drive eighteen and twenty-mule teams from the borax marsh to Mojave, ninety miles, with the trail wagon full of water barrels. Hot days the mules would go so mad for drink that the clank of the water bucket set them into an uproar of hideous, maimed noises, and a tangle of harness chains, while Salty would sit on the high seat with the sun glare heavy in his eyes, dealing out curses of pacification in a level, uninterested voice until the clamor fell off from sheer exhaustion. There was a line of shallow graves along that road; they used to count on dropping a man or two of every new gang of coolies brought out in the hot season. But when he lost his swamper, smitten without warning at the noon halt, Salty quit his job; he said it was "too durn hot." The swamper he buried by the way with stones upon him to keep the coyotes from digging him up, and seven years later I read the penciled lines on the pine headboard, still bright and unweathered.

But before that, driving up on the Mojave stage, I met Salty again crossing Indian Wells, his face from the high seat, tanned and ruddy as a harvest moon, looming through the golden dust above his eighteen mules. The land had called him.

The palpable sense of mystery in the desert air breeds fables, chiefly of lost treasure. Somewhere within its stark borders, if one believes report, is a hill strewn with nuggets; one seamed with virgin silver; an old clayey water-bed where Indians scooped up earth to make cooking pots and shaped them reeking with grains of pure gold. Old miners drifting about the desert edges, weathered into the semblance of the tawny hills, will tell you tales like these convincingly. After a little sojourn in that land you will believe them on their own account. It is a question whether it is not better to be bitten by the little horned snake of the desert that goes sidewise and strikes without coiling, than by the tradition of a lost mine.

And yet—and yet—is it not perhaps to satisfy expectation that one falls into the tragic key in writing of desertness? The more you wish of it the more you get, and in the mean time lose much of pleasantness. In that country which begins at the foot of the east slope of the Sierras and spreads out by less and less lofty hill ranges toward the Great Basin, it is possible to live with great zest, to have red blood and delicate joys, to pass and repass about one's daily performance an area that would

25

make an Atlantic seaboard State, and that with no peril, and, according to our way of thought, no particular difficulty. At any rate, it was not people who went into the desert merely to write it up who invented the fabled Hassaympa, of whose waters, if any drink, they can no more see fact as naked fact, but all radiant with the color of romance. I, who must have drunk of it in my twice seven years' wanderings, am assured that it is worth while.

For all the toll the desert takes of a man it gives compensations, deep breaths, deep sleep, and the communion of the stars. It comes upon one with new force in the pauses of the night that the Chaldeans were a desert-bred people. It is hard to escape the sense of mastery as the stars move in the wide clear heavens to risings and settings unobscured. They look large and near and palpitant; as if they moved on some stately service not needful to declare. Wheeling to their stations in the sky, they make the poor world-fret of no account. Of no account you who lie out there watching, nor the lean coyote that stands off in the scrub from you and howls and howls.

JOHN MUIR
1838–1914

A fierce advocate for the wild places of the world, John Muir's glittering essays and forceful activism contributed to the foundation of America's National Parks. Born in Scotland into a devout Christian household, he developed a precocious interest in landscape and natural history. After immigrating to Wisconsin in the late 1840s, Muir's intense feeling for nature only grew, stimulated by the bucolic life on Fountain Lake Farm. His university studies in geology and botany informed much of his later writings – for example, he was among the first to attribute a glacial origin to Yosemite Valley – and his advocacy for the preservation of nature was often bolstered by strong scientific evidence. His strict religious upbringing marked him profoundly, and his dazzling prose is everywhere animated by a searing, prophetic tenor. Despite the atmospheric force of his writing in essays such as 'A Wind-Storm in the Forests', reproduced here, Muir believed that nothing could replace the real experience of being in nature. His life and work continue to inspire millions to test this belief.

'A Wind-Storm in the Forests'

The mountain winds, like the dew and rain, sunshine and snow, are measured and bestowed with love on the forests to develop their strength and beauty. However restricted the scope of other forest influences, that of the winds is universal. The snow bends and trims the upper forests every winter, the lightning strikes a single tree here and there, while avalanches mow down thousands at a swoop as a gardener trims out a bed of flowers. But the winds go to every tree, fingering every leaf and branch and furrowed bole; not one is forgotten; the Mountain Pine towering with outstretched arms on the rugged buttresses of the icy peaks, the lowliest and most retiring tenant of the dells; they seek and find them all, caressing them tenderly, bending them in lusty exercise, stimulating their growth, plucking off a leaf or limb as required, or removing an entire tree or grove, now whispering and cooing through the branches like a sleepy child, now roaring like the ocean; the winds blessing the forests, the forests the winds, with ineffable beauty and harmony as the sure result.

After one has seen pines six feet in diameter bending like grasses before a mountain gale, and ever and anon some giant falling with a crash that shakes the hills, it seems astonishing that any, save the lowest thickset trees, could ever have found a period sufficiently stormless to establish themselves; or, once established, that they should not, sooner or later, have been blown down. But when the storm is over, and we behold the same forests tranquil again, towering fresh and unscathed in erect majesty, and consider what centuries of storms have fallen upon them since they were first planted,—hail, to break the tender seedlings; lightning, to scorch and shatter; snow, winds, and avalanches, to crush and overwhelm,—while the manifest result of all this wild storm-culture is the glorious perfection we behold; then faith in Nature's forestry is established, and we cease to deplore the violence of her most destructive gales, or of any other storm-implement whatsoever.

There are two trees in the Sierra forests that are never blown down, so long as they continue in sound health. These are the Juniper and the Dwarf Pine of the summit peaks. Their stiff, crooked roots grip the storm-beaten ledges like eagles' claws, while their lithe, cord-like branches bend round compliantly, offering but slight holds for winds, however violent. The other alpine conifers—the Needle Pine, Mountain Pine, Two-leaved Pine, and Hemlock Spruce—are never thinned out by this agent to any destructive extent, on account of their admirable toughness and the closeness of their growth. In general the same is true of the giants of the lower zones. The kingly Sugar Pine, towering aloft to a height of more than 200 feet, offers a fine mark to storm-winds; but it is not densely foliaged, and its long, horizontal arms swing round compliantly in the blast, like tresses of green, fluent algæ in a brook; while the Silver Firs in most places keep their ranks well together in united strength. The Yellow or Silver Pine is more frequently overturned than any other tree on the Sierra, because its leaves and branches form a larger mass in proportion to its height, while in many places it is planted sparsely, leaving open lanes through which storms may enter with full force. Furthermore, because it is distributed along the lower portion of the range, which was the first to be left bare on the breaking up of the ice-sheet at the close of the glacial winter, the soil it is growing upon has been longer exposed to post-glacial weathering, and consequently is in a more crumbling, decayed condition than the fresher soils farther up the range, and therefore offers a less secure anchorage for the roots.

While exploring the forest zones of Mount Shasta, I discovered the path of a hurricane strewn with thousands of pines of this species. Great and small had been uprooted or wrenched off by sheer force, making a clean gap, like that made by a snow avalanche. But hurricanes capable of doing this class of work are rare in the Sierra, and when we have explored the forests from one extremity of the range to the other, we are compelled to believe that they are the most beautiful on the face of the earth, however we may regard the agents that have made them so.

There is always something deeply exciting, not only in the sounds of winds in the woods, which exert more or less influence over every mind, but in their varied waterlike flow as manifested by the movements of the trees, especially those of the conifers. By no other trees are they rendered so extensively and impressively visible, not even by the lordly tropic palms or tree-ferns responsive to the gentlest breeze. The waving of a forest of the giant Sequoias is indescribably impressive and sublime, but the pines seem to me the best interpreters of winds. They are mighty waving goldenrods, ever in tune, singing and writing wind-music all their long century lives. Little, however, of this noble tree-waving and tree-music will you see or hear in the strictly alpine portion of the forests. The burly Juniper, whose girth sometimes more than equals its height, is about as rigid as the rocks on which it grows. The slender lash-like sprays of the Dwarf Pine stream out in wavering ripples, but the tallest and slenderest are far too unyielding to wave even in the heaviest gales. They only shake in quick, short vibrations. The Hemlock Spruce, however, and the Mountain Pine, and some of the tallest thickets of the Two-leaved species bow in storms with considerable scope and gracefulness. But it is only in the lower and middle zones that the meeting of winds and woods is to be seen in all its grandeur.

One of the most beautiful and exhilarating storms I ever enjoyed in the Sierra occurred in December, 1874, when I happened to be exploring one of the tributary valleys of the Yuba River. The sky and the ground and the trees had been thoroughly rain-washed and were dry again. The day was intensely pure, one of those incomparable bits of California winter, warm and balmy and full of white sparkling sunshine, redolent of all the purest influences of the spring, and at the same time enlivened with one of the most bracing windstorms conceivable. Instead of camping out, as I usually do, I then chanced to be stopping at the house of a friend. But when the storm began to sound, I lost no time in pushing out into the woods to enjoy it. For on such occasions Nature has always something rare to show us, and the danger to life and limb is hardly greater than one would experience crouching deprecatingly beneath a roof.

It was still early morning when I found myself fairly adrift. Delicious sunshine came pouring over the hills, lighting the tops of the pines, and setting free a steam of summery fragrance that contrasted strangely with the wild tones of the storm. The air was mottled with pine-tassels and bright green plumes, that went flashing past in the sunlight like birds pursued. But there was not the slightest dustiness, nothing less pure than leaves, and ripe pollen, and flecks of withered bracken and moss. I heard trees falling for hours at the rate of one every two or three minutes; some uprooted, partly on account of the loose, water-soaked condition of the ground; others broken straight across, where some weakness caused by fire had determined the spot. The gestures of the various trees made a delightful study. Young Sugar Pines, light and feathery as squirrel-tails, were bowing almost to the ground; while the grand old patriarchs, whose massive boles had been tried in a hundred storms, waved solemnly above them, their long, arching branches streaming fluently on the gale, and every needle thrilling and ringing and shedding off keen lances of light like a diamond. The Douglas Spruces, with long sprays drawn out in level tresses, and needles massed in a gray, shimmering glow, presented a most striking appearance as they stood in bold relief along the hilltops. The madroños in the dells, with their red bark and large glossy leaves tilted every way, reflected the sunshine in throbbing spangles like those one so often sees on the rippled surface of a glacier lake. But the Silver Pines were now the most impressively beautiful of all. Colossal spires 200 feet in height waved like supple golden-rods chanting and bowing low as if in worship, while the whole mass of their long, tremulous foliage was kindled into one continuous blaze of white sun-fire. The force of the gale was such that the most steadfast monarch of them all rocked down to its roots with a motion plainly perceptible when one leaned against it. Nature was holding high festival, and every fiber of the most rigid giants thrilled with glad excitement.

I drifted on through the midst of this passionate music and motion, across many a glen, from ridge to ridge; often halting in the lee of a rock for shelter, or to gaze and listen. Even when the grand anthem had swelled to its highest pitch, I could distinctly hear the varying tones of individual trees,—Spruce, and Fir, and Pine, and leafless Oak,—and even the infinitely gentle rustle of the withered grasses at my feet. Each was expressing itself in its own way,—singing its own song, and making its own peculiar gestures,—manifesting a richness of variety to be found in no other forest I have yet seen. The coniferous woods of Canada, and the Carolinas, and Florida, are made up of trees that resemble one another about as nearly as blades of grass, and grow close together in much the same way. Coniferous trees, in general, seldom possess individual character, such as is manifest among Oaks and Elms. But the California forests are made up of a greater number of distinct species than any other in the world. And in them we find, not only a marked differentiation into special groups, but also a marked individuality in almost every tree, giving rise to storm effects indescribably glorious.

Toward midday, after a long, tingling scramble through copses of hazel and ceanothus, I gained the summit of the highest ridge in the neighborhood; and then it occurred to me that it would be a fine thing to climb one of the trees to obtain a wider outlook and get my ear close to the Æolian music of its topmost needles. But under the circumstances the choice of a tree was a serious matter. One whose instep was not very strong seemed in danger of being blown down, or of being struck by others in case they should fall; another was branchless to a considerable height above the ground, and at the same time too large to be grasped with arms and legs in climbing; while others were not favorably situated for clear views. After cautiously casting about, I made choice of the tallest of a group of Douglas Spruces that were growing close together like a tuft of grass, no one of which seemed likely to fall unless all the rest fell with it. Though comparatively young, they were about 100 feet high, and their lithe, brushy tops were rocking and swirling in wild ecstasy. Being accustomed to climb trees in making botanical studies, I experienced no difficulty in reaching the top of this one, and never before did I enjoy so noble an exhilaration of motion. The slender tops fairly flapped and swished in the passionate torrent, bending and swirling backward and forward, round and round, tracing indescribable combinations of vertical and horizontal curves, while I clung with muscles firm braced, like a bobolink on a reed.

In its widest sweeps my tree-top described an arc of from twenty to thirty degrees, but I felt sure of its elastic temper, having seen others of the same species still more severely tried—bent almost to the ground indeed, in heavy snows—without breaking a fiber. I was therefore safe, and free to take the wind into my pulses and enjoy the excited forest from my superb outlook. The view from here must be extremely beautiful in any weather. Now my eye roved over the piny hills and dales as over fields of waving grain, and felt the light running in ripples and broad swelling undulations across the valleys from ridge to ridge, as the shining foliage was stirred by corresponding waves of air. Oftentimes these waves of reflected light would break up suddenly into a kind of beaten foam, and again, after chasing one another in regular order, they would seem to bend forward in concentric curves, and disappear on some hillside, like sea-waves on a shelving shore. The quantity of light reflected from the bent needles was so great as to make whole groves appear as if covered with snow, while the black shadows beneath the trees greatly enhanced the effect of the silvery splendor.

Excepting only the shadows there was nothing somber in all this wild sea of pines. On the contrary, notwithstanding this was the winter season, the colors were remarkably beautiful. The shafts of the pine and libocedrus were brown and purple, and most of the foliage was well tinged with yellow;

the laurel groves, with the pale undersides of their leaves turned upward, made masses of gray; and then there was many a dash of chocolate color from clumps of manzanita, and jet of vivid crimson from the bark of the madroños, while the ground on the hillsides, appearing here and there through openings between the groves, displayed masses of pale purple and brown.

The sounds of the storm corresponded gloriously with this wild exuberance of light and motion. The profound bass of the naked branches and boles booming like waterfalls; the quick, tense vibrations of the pine-needles, now rising to a shrill, whistling hiss, now falling to a silky murmur; the rustling of laurel groves in the dells, and the keen metallic click of leaf on leaf—all this was heard in easy analysis when the attention was calmly bent.

The varied gestures of the multitude were seen to fine advantage, so that one could recognize the different species at a distance of several miles by this means alone, as well as by their forms and colors, and the way they reflected the light. All seemed strong and comfortable, as if really enjoying the storm, while responding to its most enthusiastic greetings. We hear much nowadays concerning the universal struggle for existence, but no struggle in the common meaning of the word was manifest here; no recognition of danger by any tree; no deprecation; but rather an invincible gladness as remote from exultation as from fear.

I kept my lofty perch for hours, frequently closing my eyes to enjoy the music by itself, or to feast quietly on the delicious fragrance that was streaming past. The fragrance of the woods was less marked than that produced during warm rain, when so many balsamic buds and leaves are steeped like tea; but, from the chafing of resiny branches against each other, and the incessant attrition of myriads of needles, the gale was spiced to a very tonic degree. And besides the fragrance from these local sources there were traces of scents brought from afar. For this wind came first from the sea, rubbing against its fresh, briny waves, then distilled through the redwoods, threading rich ferny gulches, and spreading itself in broad undulating currents over many a flower-enameled ridge of the coast mountains, then across the golden plains, up the purple foot-hills, and into these piny woods with the varied incense gathered by the way.

Winds are advertisements of all they touch, however much or little we may be able to read them; telling their wanderings even by their scents alone. Mariners detect the flowery perfume of land-winds far at sea, and sea-winds carry the fragrance of dulse and tangle far inland, where it is quickly recognized, though mingled with the scents of a thousand land-flowers. As an illustration of this, I may tell here that I breathed sea-air on the Firth of Forth, in Scotland, while a boy; then was taken to Wisconsin, where I remained nineteen years; then, without in all this time having breathed one breath of the sea, I walked quietly, alone, from the middle of the Mississippi Valley to the Gulf of Mexico, on a botanical excursion, and while in Florida, far from the coast, my attention wholly bent on the splendid tropical vegetation about me, I suddenly recognized a sea-breeze, as it came sifting through the palmettos and blooming vine-tangles, which at once awakened and set free a thousand dormant associations, and made me a boy again in Scotland, as if all the intervening years had been annihilated.

Most people like to look at mountain rivers, and bear them in mind; but few care to look at the winds, though far more beautiful and sublime, and though they become at times about as visible as flowing water. When the north winds in winter are making upward sweeps over the curving summits of the High Sierra, the fact is sometimes published with flying snow-banners a mile long.

Those portions of the winds thus embodied can scarce be wholly invisible, even to the darkest imagination. And when we look around over an agitated forest, we may see something of the wind that stirs it, by its effects upon the trees. Yonder it descends in a rush of water-like ripples, and sweeps over the bending pines from hill to hill. Nearer, we see detached plumes and leaves, now speeding by on level currents, now whirling in eddies, or, escaping over the edges of the whirls, soaring aloft on grand, upswelling domes of air, or tossing on flame-like crests. Smooth, deep currents, cascades, falls, and swirling eddies, sing around every tree and leaf, and over all the varied topography of the region with telling changes of form, like mountain rivers conforming to the features of their channels.

After tracing the Sierra streams from their fountains to the plains, marking where they bloom white in falls, glide in crystal plumes, surge gray and foam-filled in boulder-choked gorges, and slip through the woods in long, tranquil reaches—after thus learning their language and forms in detail, we may at length hear them chanting all together in one grand anthem, and comprehend them all in clear inner vision, covering the range like lace. But even this spectacle is far less sublime and not a whit more substantial than what we may behold of these storm-streams of air in the mountain woods.

We all travel the milky way together, trees and men; but it never occurred to me until this storm-day, while swinging in the wind, that trees are travelers, in the ordinary sense. They make many journeys, not extensive ones, it is true; but our own little journeys, away and back again, are only little more than tree-wavings—many of them not so much.

When the storm began to abate, I dismounted and sauntered down through the calming woods. The storm-tones died away, and, turning toward the east, I beheld the countless hosts of the forests hushed and tranquil, towering above one another on the slopes of the hills like a devout audience. The setting sun filled them with amber light, and seemed to say, while they listened, "My peace I give unto you."

As I gazed on the impressive scene, all the so-called ruin of the storm was forgotten, and never before did these noble woods appear so fresh, so joyous, so immortal.

ISABELLA BIRD
1831–1904

Isabella Bird was a celebrated writer and seasoned explorer. A sickly child, she was pushed towards an active life to combat her illness. She learned to ride, row, and, later, to explore. A trip to the United States in 1854 led to her first book, amusing descriptive letters collected as *The Englishwoman in America* (1856). More travel followed – to Australia, Hawaii, Japan and Korea – and with almost every journey, another book was born. In 1889, at nearly sixty years old, Bird decided that her earlier trips had been mere pleasure-seeking. To remedy the fault, she studied medicine and left for India as a missionary. She went on to travel extensively in Tibet, Iraq, Iran and Morocco. She died in Edinburgh, Scotland, while planning a trip to China. Her best-known work, *A Lady's Life in the Rocky Mountains* (1879), details an 800-mile trip through Colorado on horseback. The letter reproduced here shows her arch wit, her unyielding energy and her enthusiasm for adventure.

from *A Lady's Life in the Rocky Mountains*

It is not easy to sit down to write after ten hours of hard riding, especially in a cabin full of people, and wholesome fatigue may make my letter flat when it ought to be enthusiastic. I was awake all night at Longmount owing to the stifling heat, and got up nervous and miserable, ready to give up the thought of coming here, but the sunrise over the plains, and the wonderful red of the Rocky Mountains, as they reflected the eastern sky, put spirit into me. The landlord had got a horse, but could not give any satisfactory assurances of his being quiet, and being much shaken by my fall at Canyon, I earnestly wished that the *Greeley Tribune* had not given me a reputation for horsemanship, which had preceded me here. The young men who were to escort me "seemed very innocent," he said, but I have not arrived at his meaning yet. When the horse appeared in the street at 8.30, I saw, to my dismay, a high-bred, beautiful creature, stable-kept, with arched neck, quivering nostrils, and restless ears and eyes. My pack, as on Hawaii, was strapped behind the Mexican saddle, and my canvas bag hung on the horn, but the horse did not look fit to carry "gear," and seemed to require two men to hold and coax him. There were many loafers about, and I shrank from going out and mounting in my old Hawaiian riding-dress, though Dr. and Mrs. H. assured me that I looked quite "insignificant and unnoticeable." We got away at nine with repeated injunctions from the landlord in the words, "Oh, you should be heroic!"

The sky was cloudless, and a deep brilliant blue, and though the sun was hot the air was fresh and bracing. The ride for glory and delight I shall label along with one to Hanalei, and another to Mauna Kea, Hawaii. I felt better quite soon; the horse in gait and temper turned out perfection—all spring and spirit, elastic in his motion, walking fast and easily, and cantering with a light, graceful swing as soon as one pressed the reins on his neck, a blithe, joyous animal, to whom a day among the mountains seemed a pleasant frolic. So gentle he was, that when I got off and walked he followed me without being led, and without needing any one to hold him he allowed me to mount on either side. In addition to the charm of his movements he has the cat-like sure-footedness of a Hawaiian horse, and fords rapid and rough-bottomed rivers, and gallops among stones and stumps, and down steep hills, with equal security. I could have ridden him a hundred miles as easily as thirty. We have only been together two days, yet we are firm friends, and thoroughly understand each other. I should not require another companion on a long mountain tour. All his ways are those of an animal brought up without curb, whip, or spur, trained by the voice, and used only to kindness, as is happily the case with the majority of horses in the Western States. Consequently, unless they are *broncos*, they exercise their intelligence for your advantage, and do their work rather as friends than as machines.

I soon began not only to feel better, but to be exhilarated with the delightful motion. The sun was behind us, and puffs of a cool elastic air came down from the glorious mountains in front. We cantered across six miles of prairie, and then reached the beautiful canyon of the St. Vrain, which, towards its mouth, is a narrow, fertile, wooded valley, through which a bright rapid river, which we forded many times, hurries along, with twists and windings innumerable. Ah, how brightly its ripples danced in the glittering sunshine, and how musically its waters murmured like the streams of windward Hawaii! We lost our way over and over again, though the "innocent" young men had been there before; indeed, it would require some talent to master the intricacies of that devious trail, but settlers making hay always appeared in the nick of time to put us on the right track. Very fair it was, after the brown and burning plains, and the variety was endless. Cotton-wood trees were green and bright, aspens shivered in golden tremulousness, wild grape-vines trailed their lemon-coloured foliage along the ground, and the Virginia creeper hung its crimson sprays here and there, lighting up green and gold into glory. Sometimes from under the cool and bowery shade of the coloured tangle we passed into the cool St. Vrain, and then were wedged between its margin and lofty cliffs and terraces of incredibly staring, fantastic rocks, lined, patched, and splashed with carmine, vermilion, greens of all tints, blue, yellow, orange, violet, deep crimson, colouring that no artist would dare to represent, and of which, in sober prose, I scarcely dare tell. Long's wonderful peaks, which hitherto had gleamed above the green, now disappeared, to be seen no more for twenty miles. We entered on an ascending valley, where the gorgeous hues of the rocks were intensified by the blue gloom of the pitch-pines, and then taking a track to the northwest, we left the softer world behind, and all traces of man and his works, and plunged into the Rocky Mountains.

There were wonderful ascents then up which I led my horse: wild fantastic views opening up continually, a recurrence of surprises; the air keener

47

and purer with every mile, the sensation of loneliness more singular. A tremendous ascent among rocks and pines to a height of 9000 feet brought us to a passage seven feet wide through a wall of rock, with an abrupt descent of 2000 feet, and a yet higher ascent beyond. I never saw anything so strange as looking back. It was a single gigantic ridge which we had passed through, standing up knife-like, built up entirely of great brick-shaped masses of bright-red rock, some of them as large as the Royal Institution, Edinburgh, piled one on another by Titans. Pitch-pines grew out of their crevices, but there was not a vestige of soil. Beyond, wall beyond wall of similar construction, and range above range, rose into the blue sky. Fifteen miles more over great ridges, along passes dark with shadow, and so narrow that we had to ride in the beds of the streams which had excavated them, round the bases of colossal pyramids of rock crested with pines, up into fair upland "parks," scarlet in patches with the poison oak, parks so beautifully arranged by nature that I momentarily expected to come upon some stately mansion, but that afternoon crested blue jays and chipmonks had them all to themselves. Here, in the early morning, deer, bighorn, and the stately elk, come down to feed, and there, in the night, prowl and growl the Rocky Mountain lion, the grizzly bear, and the cowardly wolf. There were chasms of immense depth, dark with the indigo gloom of pines, and mountains with snow gleaming on their splintered crests, loveliness to bewilder and grandeur to awe, and still streams and shady pools, and cool depths of shadow; mountains again, dense with pines, among which patches of aspen gleamed like gold; valleys where the yellow cottonwood mingled with the crimson oak, and so, on and on through the lengthening shadows, till the trail, which in places had been hardly legible, became well defined, and we entered a long gulch with broad swellings of grass belted with pines.

A very pretty mare, hobbled, was feeding; a collie dog barked at us, and among the scrub, not far from the track, there was a rude, black log cabin, as rough as it could be to be a shelter at all, with smoke coming out of the roof and window. We diverged towards it; it mattered not that it was the home, or rather den, of a notorious "ruffian" and "desperado." One of my companions had disappeared hours before, the remaining one was a town-bred youth. I longed to speak to some one who loved the mountains. I called the hut a *den*—it looked like the den of a wild beast. The big dog lay outside it in a threatening attitude and growled.

The mud roof was covered with lynx, beaver, and other furs laid out to dry, beaver paws were pinned out on the logs, a part of the carcass of a deer hung at one end of the cabin, a skinned beaver lay in front of a heap of peltry just within the door, and antlers of deer, old horseshoes, and offal of many animals, lay about the den. Roused by the growling of the dog, his owner came out, a broad, thickset man, about the middle height, with an old cap on his head, and wearing a grey hunting-suit much the worse for wear (almost falling to pieces, in fact), a digger's scarf knotted round his waist, a knife in his belt, and "a bosom friend," a revolver, sticking out of the breast-pocket of his coat; his feet, which were very small, were bare, except for some dilapidated moccasins made of horse hide. The marvel was how his clothes hung together, and on him. The scarf round his waist must have had something to do with it. His face was remarkable. He is a man about forty-five, and must have been strikingly hand-some. He has large grey-blue eyes, deeply set, with well-marked eyebrows, a handsome aquiline nose, and a very handsome mouth. His face was smooth-shaven except for a dense moustache and imperial. Tawny hair, in thin uncared-for curls, fell from under his hunter's cap and over his collar. One eye was entirely gone, and the loss made one side of the face repulsive, while the other might have been modelled in marble. "Desperado" was written in large letters all over him. I almost repented of having sought his acquaintance. His first impulse was to swear at the dog, but on seeing a lady he contented himself with kicking him, and coming up to me he raised his cap, showing as he did so a magnificently-formed brow and head, and in a cultured tone of voice asked if there were anything he could do for me? I asked for some water, and he brought some in a battered tin, gracefully apologising for not having anything more presentable. We entered into conversation, and as he spoke I forgot both his reputation and appearance, for his manner was that of a chivalrous gentleman, his accent refined, and his language easy and elegant. I inquired about some beavers' paws which were drying, and in a moment they hung on the horn of my saddle. *Apropos* of the wild animals of the region, he told me that the loss of his eye was owing to a recent encounter with a grizzly bear, which, after giving him a death hug, tearing him all over, breaking his arm and scratching out his eye, had left him for dead. As we rode away, for the sun was sinking, he said, courteously, "You are not an American. I know from your voice that you are a countrywoman of mine. I hope you will allow me the pleasure of calling on you."* This man, known through the Territories and beyond them as "Rocky Mountain Jim," or, more briefly, as "Mountain Jim," is one of the famous scouts of the Plains, and is the original of some daring portraits in fiction concerning Indian frontier warfare. So far as I have at present heard, he is a man for whom there is now no room, for the time for blows and blood in this part of Colorado is past, and the fame of many daring exploits is sullied by crimes which are not easily forgiven here. He now has a "squatter's claim," but makes his living as a trapper, and is a complete child of the mountains. Of his genius and chivalry to women there does not appear to be any doubt; but he is a desperate character, and is subject to "ugly fits," when people think it best to avoid him. It is here regarded as an evil that he has located himself at the mouth of the only entrance to

* Of this unhappy man, who was shot nine months later within two miles of his cabin, I write in the subsequent letters only as he appeared to me. His life, without doubt, was deeply stained with crimes and vices, and his reputation for ruffianism was a deserved one. But in my intercourse with him I saw more of his nobler instincts than of the darker parts of his character, which, unfortunately for himself and others, showed itself in its worst colours at the time of his tragic end. It was not until after I left Colorado, not indeed until after his death, that I heard of the worst points of his character.

the Park, for he is dangerous with his pistols, and it would be safer if he were not here. His besetting sin is indicated in the verdict pronounced on him by my host: "When he's sober Jim's a perfect gentleman; but when he's had liquor he's the most awful ruffian in Colorado."

From the ridge on which this gulch terminates, at a height of 9000 feet, we saw at last Estes Park, lying 1500 feet below in the glory of the setting sun, an irregular basin, lighted up by the bright waters of the rushing Thompson, guarded by sentinel mountains of fantastic shape and monstrous size, with Long's Peak rising above them all in unapproachable grandeur, while the Snowy Range, with its outlying spurs heavily timbered, come down upon the Park slashed by stupendous canyons lying deep in purple gloom. The rushing river was blood-red, Long's Peak was aflame, the glory of the glowing heaven was given back from earth. Never, nowhere, have I seen anything to equal the view into Estes Park. The mountains "of the land which is very far off" are very near now, but the near is more glorious than the far, and reality than dreamland. The mountain fever seized me, and, giving my tireless horse one encouraging word, he dashed at full gallop over a mile of smooth sward at delirious speed. But I was hungry, and the air was frosty, and I was wondering what the prospects of food and shelter were in this enchanted region, when we came suddenly upon a small lake, close to which was a very trim-looking log cabin, with a flat mud roof, with four smaller ones; picturesquely dotted about near it, two *corrals*,* a long shed, in front of which a steer was being killed, a log-dairy with a water-wheel, some hay-piles, and various evidences of comfort; and two men, on serviceable horses, were just bringing in some tolerable cows to be milked. A short, pleasant-looking man ran up to me and shook hands gleefully, which surprised me; but he has since told me that in the evening light he thought I was "Mountain Jim, dressed up as a woman!" I recognised in him a countryman, and he introduced himself as Griffith Evans, a Welshman from the slate quarries near Llanberis. When the cabin-door was opened I saw a good-sized log room, unchinked, however, with windows of infamous glass, looking two ways; a rough stone fireplace, in which pine logs, half as large as I am, were burning; a boarded floor, a round table, two rocking-chairs, a carpet-covered

* A *corral* is a fenced enclosure for cattle. This word, with *bronco*, *ranch*, and a few others, are adaptations from the Spanish, and are used as extensively throughout California and the Territories as is the Spanish or Mexican saddle.

backwoods couch; and skins, Indian bows and arrows, wampum belts, and antlers, fitly decorated the rough walls, and equally fitly rifles were stuck up in the corners. Seven men, smoking, were lying about on the floor, a sick man lay on the couch, and a middle-aged lady sat at the table writing. I went out again and asked Evans if he could take me in, expecting nothing better than a shakedown; but, to my joy, he told me he could give me a cabin to myself, two minutes' walk from his own. So in this glorious upper world, with the mountain pines behind and the clear lake in front, in the "blue hollow at the foot of Long's Peak," at a height of 7500 feet, where the hoar frost crisps the grass every night of the year, I have found far more than I ever dared to hope for.

BIRDS, INSECTS, ANIMALS

GILBERT WHITE
1720–1793

Gilbert White, parson-naturalist, was born and
died in Selborne, Hampshire. Though he was edu-
cated at Oxford and held several curacies in
Wiltshire and Hampshire, it is with Selborne that
he is forever associated. In dozens of sharply
observed and carefully written letters to two fellow
English naturalists, White's *The Natural History
and Antiquities of Selborne* (1789) details the flora
and fauna he observed on long rambles through
his parish and its environs. Widely considered the
founding document of modern nature writing,
these letters demonstrate White's limitless curiosity, his loving attention and his undying belief in
the beauty and significance of the natural world, be
it in the life of the earthworm or the lark, the tor-
toise, or, as in the letter here, the swift.

from *The Natural History and Antiquities of Selborne*

LETTER XXI
TO THE SAME

SELBORNE, *Sept. 28, 1774.*

DEAR SIR,—As the *swift* or *black-martin* is the largest of the *British hirundines*, so it is undoubtedly the latest comer. For I remember but one instance of it's appearing before the last week in *April*; and in some of our late frosty, harsh springs, it has not been seen till the beginning of *May*. This species usually arrives in pairs.

The swift, like the sand-martin, is very defective in architecture, making no crust, or shell, for it's nest; but forming it of dry grasses and feathers, very rudely and inartificially put together. With all my attention to these birds, I have never been able once to discover one in the act of collecting or carrying in materials: so that I have suspected (since their nests are exactly the same) that they sometimes usurp upon the house-sparrows, and expel them, as sparrows do the house and sand-martin; well remembering that I have seen them squabbling together at the entrance of their holes; and the sparrows up in arms, and much disconcerted at these intruders. And yet I am assured, by a nice observer in such matters, that they do collect feathers for their nests in *Andalusia*, and that he has shot them with such materials in their mouths.

Swifts, like sand-martins, carry on the business of nidification quite in the dark, in crannies of castles, and towers, and steeples, and upon the tops of the walls of churches under the roof; and therefore cannot be so narrowly watched as those species that build more openly: but, from what I could ever observe, they begin nesting about the middle of *May*; and I have remarked, from eggs taken, that they have sat hard by the ninth of *June*. In general they haunt tall buildings, churches, and steeples, and breed only in such: yet in this village some pairs frequent the lowest and meanest cottages, and educate their young under those thatched roofs. We remember but one instance where they breed out of buildings, and that is in the sides of a deep chalk-pit near the town of *Odiham*, in this county, where we have seen many pairs entering the crevices, and skimming and squeaking round the precipices.

As I have regarded these amusive birds with no small attention, if I should advance something new and peculiar with respect to them, and different from all other birds, I might perhaps be credited;

especially as my assertion is the result of many years exact observation. The fact that I would advance is, that swifts *tread*, or copulate, on the wing: and I would wish any nice observer, that is startled at this supposition, to use his own eyes, and I think he will soon be convinced. In another *class* of animals, *viz.*, the *insect*, nothing is so common as to see the different species of many genera in conjunction as they fly. The swift is almost continually on the wing; and as it never settles on the ground, on trees, or roofs, would seldom find opportunity for amorous rites, was it not enabled to indulge them in the air. If any person would watch these birds of a fine morning in *May*, as they are sailing round at a great height from the ground, he would see, every now and then, one drop on the back of another, and both of them sink down together for many fathoms with a loud piercing shriek. This I take to be the juncture when the business of generation is carrying on.

As the swift eats, drinks, collects materials for it's nest, and, as it seems, propagates on the wing, it appears to live more in the air than any other bird, and to perform all functions there save those of sleeping and incubation.

This *hirundo* differs widely from it's congeners in laying invariably but *two* eggs at a time, which are milk-white, long, and peaked at the small end; whereas the other species lay at each brood from *four* to *six*. It is a most alert bird, rising very early, and retiring to roost very late; and is on the wing in the height of summer at least sixteen hours. In the longest days it does not withdraw to rest till a quarter before nine in the evening, being the latest of all day birds. Just before they retire whole groups of them assemble high in the air, and squeak, and shoot about with wonderful rapidity. But this bird is never so much alive as in sultry thundry weather, when it expresses great alacrity, and calls forth all it's powers. In hot mornings, several, getting together in little parties, dash round the steeples and churches, squeaking as they go in a very clamorous manner: these, by nice observers, are supposed to be males serenading their sitting hens; and not without reason, since they seldom squeak till they come close to the walls or eaves, and since those within utter at the same time a little inward note of complacency.

When the hen has sat hard all day, she rushes forth just as it is almost dark, and stretches and relieves her weary limbs, and snatches a scanty meal for a few minutes, and then returns to her duty of incubation. Swifts, when wantonly and cruelly shot while

63

they have young, discover a little lump of insects in their mouths, which they pouch and hold under their tongue. In general they feed in a much higher district than the other species; a proof that gnats and other insects do also abound to a considerable height in the air: they also range to vast distances; since loco-motion is no labour to them who are endowed with such wonderful powers of wing. Their powers seem to be in proportion to their leavers; and their wings are longer in proportion than those of almost any other bird. When they mute, or ease themselves in flight, they raise their wings, and make them meet over their backs.

At some certain times in the summer I had remarked that swifts were hawking very low for hours together over pools and streams; and could not help inquiring into the object of their pursuit that induced them to descend so much below their usual range. After some trouble I found that they were taking *phryganeæ*, *ephemeræ*, and *libellulæ* (cadew-flies, may-flies, and dragon-flies), that were just emerged out of their aurelia state. I then no longer wondered that they should be so willing to stoop for a prey that afforded them such plentiful and succulent nourishment.

They bring out their young about the middle or latter end of *July*: but as these never become perchers, nor, that ever I could discern, are fed on the wing by their dams, the coming forth of the young is not so notorious as in the other species.

On the thirtieth of last *June* I untiled the eaves of a house where many pairs build, and found in each nest only *two* squab, naked *pulli*: on the eighth of *July* I repeated the same inquiry, and found that they had made very little progress towards a fledged state, but were still naked and helpless. From whence we may conclude that birds whose way of life keeps them perpetually on the wing would not be able to quit their nest till the end of the month. Swallows and martins, that have numerous families, are continually feeding them every two or three minutes; while swifts, that have but two young to maintain, are much at their leisure, and do not attend on their nests for hours together.

Sometimes they pursue and strike at hawks that come in their way; but not with that vehemence and fury that swallows express on the same occasion. They are out all day long in wet days, feeding about, and disregarding still rain: from whence two things may be gathered; first, that many insects abide high in the air, even in rain; and next, that the feathers of these birds must be well preened to resist so much wet. Windy, and particularly windy weather with heavy showers, they dislike; and on such days withdraw, and are scarce ever seen.

There is a circumstance respecting the *colour* of swifts, which seems not to be unworthy our attention. When they arrive in the spring they are all over of a glossy, dark soot-colour, except their chins, which are white; but, by being all day long in the sun and air, they become quite weather-beaten and bleached before they depart, and yet they return glossy again in the spring. Now, if they pursue the sun into lower latitudes, as some suppose, in order to enjoy a perpetual summer, why do they not return bleached? Do they not rather perhaps retire to rest for a season, and at that juncture moult and change their feathers, since all other birds are known to moult soon after the season of breeding?

Swifts are very anomalous in many particulars, dissenting from all their congeners not only in the number of their young, but in breeding but *once* in a summer; whereas all the other *British hirundines* breed invariably *twice*. It is past all doubt that swifts can breed but once, since they withdraw in a short time after the flight of their young, and some time before their congeners bring out their second broods. We may here remark that, as swifts breed but *once* in a summer, and only *two* at a time, and the other *hirundines twice*, the latter, who lay

66

from four to six eggs, increase at an average five times as fast as the former.

But in nothing are swifts more singular than in their early retreat. They retire, as to the main body of them, by the tenth of *August*, and sometimes a few days sooner: and every straggler invariably withdraws by the twentieth, while their congeners, all of them, stay till the beginning of *October*; many of them all through that month and some occasionally to the beginning of *November*. This early retreat is mysterious and wonderful, since that time is often the sweetest season in the year. But, what is more extraordinary, they begin to retire still earlier in the most southerly parts of *Andalusia*, where they can be in no ways influenced by any defect of heat, or, as one might suppose, defect of food. Are they regulated in their motions with us by a failure of food, or by a propensity to moulting, or by a disposition to rest after so rapid a life, or by what? This is one of those incidents in natural history that not only baffles our searches, but almost eludes our guesses!

These hirundines never perch on trees or roofs, and so never congregate with their congeners. They are fearless while haunting their nesting places, and are not to be scared with a gun; and are often beaten down with poles and cudgels as they stoop to go under the eaves. Swifts are much infested with those pests to the genus called *hippoboscæ hirundinis*; and often wriggle and scratch themselves, in their flight, to get rid of that clinging annoyance.

Swifts are no songsters, and have only one harsh screaming note; yet there are ears to which it is not displeasing, from an agreeable association of ideas, since that note never occurs but in the most lovely summer weather.

They never can settle on the ground but through accident; and when down, can hardly rise, on account of the shortness of their legs and the length of their wings: neither can they walk, but only crawl; but they have a strong grasp with their feet, by which they cling to walls. Their bodies being flat they can enter a very narrow crevice; and where they cannot pass on their bellies they will turn up edgewise.

The particular formation of the foot discriminates the swift from all the *British hirundines*; and indeed from all other known birds, the *hirundo melba*, or great white-bellied swift of *Gibraltar*, excepted; for it is so disposed as to carry "*omnes quatuor digitos anticos*"—all it's four toes forward; besides, the least toe, which should be the back-toe, consists of one bone alone, and the other three only of two apiece. A construction most rare and peculiar, but nicely adapted to the purposes in which their feet are employed. This, and some peculiarities attending the nostrils and under mandible, have induced a discerning naturalist to suppose that this *species* might constitute a genus *per se*.

In *London* a party of swifts frequents the *Tower*, playing and feeding over the river just below the bridge: others haunt some of the churches of the *Borough*, next the fields; but do not venture, like the *house-martin*, into the close crowded part of the town.

The *Swedes* have bestowed a very pertinent name on this swallow, calling it *ring swala*, from the perpetual *rings* or circles that it takes round the scene of it's nidification.

Swifts feed on *coleoptera*, or small beetles with hard cases over their wings, as well as on the softer insects; but it does not appear how they can procure gravel to grind their food, as swallows do, since they never settle on the ground. Young ones, overrun with *hipposcæ*, are sometimes found, under their nests, fallen to the ground; the number of vermin rendering their abode insupportable any longer. They frequent in this village several abject cottages; yet a succession still haunts the same unlikely roofs: a good proof this that the same birds return to the same spots. As they must stoop very low to get up under these humble eaves, cats lie in wait, and sometimes catch them on the wing.

On the 5th of *July*, 1775, I again untiled part of a roof over the nest of a swift. The dam sat in the nest; but so strongly was she affected by natural στοργή for her brood, which she supposed to be in danger, that, regardless of her own safety, she would not stir, but lay sullenly by them, permitting herself to be taken in hand. The squab young we brought down and placed on the grass-plot, where they tumbled about, and were as helpless as a new-born child. While we contemplated their naked bodies, their unwieldy disproportioned abdomina, and their heads, too heavy for their necks to support, we could not but wonder when we reflected that these shiftless beings in a little more than a fortnight would be able to dash through the air almost with the inconceivable swiftness of a meteor; and perhaps in their emigration, must traverse vast continents and oceans as distant as the equator. So soon does Nature advance small birds to their ἡλικία, or state of perfection; while the progressive growth of men and large quadrupeds is slow and tedious!

I am, &c.

JOHN JAMES AUDUBON
1785–1851

A gifted draughtsman with a passionate interest in birdlife, John James Audubon never felt at ease in the seafaring career his father, a French naval officer, intended for him. In 1803, to avoid conscription in the Napoleonic Wars, Audubon immigrated to the United States, where, in his leisure hours, he began to study the birds of America. Although periodically interrupted by illness, debt and eclectic commercial endeavours, Audubon doggedly pursued his ornithological passion. To better understand birds, he learned anatomy, taxidermy and methods of scientific research. To better represent them, he studied painting and illustration. To better promote them, he opened a museum of natural history. This patient preparation resulted in his stunning elephant folio, *The Birds of America* (1827–38), which made him famous around the world. Audubon's spectacular illustrations show birdlife at its most dramatic, in fight or flight, and at its most tender, in mating or caring for the young. The *Ornithological Biography*

(1831–39), excerpted here, accompanied these images, and was co-written by the Scottish ornithologist William MacGillivray (1796–1852).

'The Raven', from *Ornithological Biography*

In the United States, the Raven is in some measure a migratory bird, individuals retiring to the extreme south during severe winters, but returning towards the Middle, Western, and Northern Districts, at the first indications of milder weather. A few are known to breed in the mountainous portions of South Carolina, but instances of this kind are rare, and are occasioned merely by the security afforded by inaccessible precipices, in which they may rear their young. Their usual places of resort are the mountains, the abrupt banks of rivers, the rocky shores of lakes, and the cliffs of thinly-peopled or deserted islands. It is in such places that these birds must be watched and examined, before one can judge of their natural habits, as manifested amid their freedom from the dread of their most dangerous enemy, the lord of the creation.

There, through the clear and rarified atmosphere, the Raven spreads his glossy wings and tail, and, as he onward sails, rises higher and higher each bold sweep that he makes, as if conscious that the nearer he approaches the sun, the more splendent will become the tints of his plumage. Intent on convincing his mate of the fervour and constancy of his love, he now gently glides beneath her, floats in the buoyant air, or sails by her side. Would that I could describe to you, reader, the many musical inflections by means of which they hold converse during these amatory excursions! These sounds doubtless express their pure conjugal feelings, confirmed and rendered more intense by long years of happiness in each other's society. In this manner they may recall the pleasing remembrance of their youthful days, recount the events of their life, express the pleasure they have enjoyed, and perhaps conclude with humble prayer to the Author of their being for a continuation of it.

Now, their matins are over; the happy pair are seen to glide towards the earth in spiral lines; they alight on the boldest summit of a rock, so high that you can scarcely judge of their actual size; they approach each other, their bills meet, and caresses are exchanged as tender as those of the gentle Turtle Dove. Far beneath, wave after wave dashes in foam against the impregnable sides of the rocky tower, the very aspect of which would be terrific to almost any other creatures than the sable pair, which for years have resorted to it, to rear the dearly-cherished fruits of their connubial love. Midway between them and the boiling waters, some shelving ledge conceals their eyry. To it they now betake themselves, to see what damage it has sustained from the peltings of the winter tempests. Off they fly to the distant woods for fresh materials with which to repair the breach; or on the plain they collect the hair and fur of quadrupeds; or from the sandy beach pick up the weeds that have been washed there. By degrees, the nest is enlarged and trimmed, and when every thing has been rendered clean and comfortable, the female deposits her eggs, and begins to sit upon them, while her brave and affectionate mate protects and feeds her, and at intervals takes her place.

All around is now silent, save the hoarse murmur of the waves, or the whistling sounds produced by the flight of the waterfowl travelling towards the northern regions. At length the young burst the shell, when the careful parents, after congratulating each other on the happy event, disgorge some half-macerated food, which they deposit in their tender mouths. Should the most daring adventurer of the air approach, he is attacked with fury and repelled. As the young grow up, they are urged to be careful and silent:—a single false movement might precipitate them into the abyss below; a single cry during the absence of their parents might bring upon them the remorseless claws of the swift Peregrine or Jerfalcon. The old birds themselves seem to improve in care, diligence, and activity, varying their course when returning to their home, and often entering it when unexpected. The young are now seen to stand on the edge of the nest; they flap their wings, and at length take courage and fly to some more commodious and not distant lodgment. Gradually they become able to follow their parents abroad, and at length search for maintenance in their company, and that of others, until the period of breeding arrives, when they separate in pairs, and disperse.

Notwithstanding all the care of the Raven, his nest is invaded where-ever it is found. His usefulness is forgotten, his faults are remembered and multiplied by imagination; and whenever he presents himself he is shot at, because from time immemorial ignorance, prejudice, and destructiveness have operated on the mind of man to his detriment. Men will peril their lives to reach his nest, assisted by ropes and poles, alleging merely that he has killed one of their numerous sheep or lambs. Some say they destroy the Raven because he is black; others, because his croaking is unpleasant and ominous! Unfortunate truly are the young ones that are carried home to become the wretched pets of some ill-brought-up child! For my part, I admire the Raven, because I see much in him calculated to excite our wonder. It is true that he may sometimes hasten the death of a half-starved sheep, or destroy a weakly lamb; he may eat the eggs of other birds, or occasionally steal from the farmer some of those which he calls his own; young fowls also afford precious morsels to himself and his progeny;—but how many sheep, lambs, and fowls, are saved through his agency! The more intelligent of our farmers are well aware that the Raven destroys numberless insects, grubs, and worms; that he kills mice, moles, and rats, when-ever he can find them; that he will seize the weasel, the young opossum, and the skunk; that, with the perseverance of a cat, he will watch the burrows of foxes, and pounce on the cubs; our farmers also are fully aware that he apprises them of the wolf's prowlings around their yard, and that he never intrudes on their corn fields except to benefit them;—yes, good reader, the farmer knows all this well, but he also knows his power, and, interfere as you may, with tale of pity or of truth, the bird is a Raven, and, as LAFONTAINE has aptly and most truly said, "La loi du plus fort est toujours la meil-leure!"

[...]

The Raven may be said to be of a social dispos-ition, for, after the breeding season, flocks of forty, fifty, or more, may sometimes be seen, as I observed on the coast of Labrador, and on the Missouri. When domesticated, and treated with kindness, it becomes attached to its owner, and will follow him about with all the familiarity of a confiding friend. It is capable of imitating the human voice, so that individuals have sometimes been taught to enunciate a few words with great distinctness.

On the ground the Raven walks in a stately manner, its motions exhibiting a kind of thoughtful consideration, almost amounting to gravity. While walking it frequently moves up its wings as if to keep their muscles in action. I never knew an instance of their roosting in the woods, although they frequently alight on trees, to which they sometimes resort for the purpose of procuring nuts and other fruits. They usually betake themselves at night to high rocks, in situations protected from the northerly winds. Possessing to all appearance the faculty of judging of the coming weather, they remove from the higher, wild and dreary districts where they breed, into the low lands, at the approach of winter, when they are frequently seen along the shores of the sea, collecting the garbage that has been cast to land, or picking up the shellfish as the tide retires. They are vigilant, industrious, and, when the safety of their young or nest is at stake, courageous, driving away hawks and eagles whenever they happen to come near, although in no ease do they venture to attack man. Indeed, it is extremely difficult to get within shot of an old Raven. I have more than once been only a few yards from one while it was sitting on its eggs, having attained this proximity by creeping cautiously to the overhanging edge of a precipice; but the moment the bird perceived me, it would fly off apparently in much confusion. They are so cunning and wary, that they can seldom be caught in a trap; and they will watch one intended for a fox, a wolf, or a bear, until one of these animals comes up, and is taken, when they will go to it and eat the alluring bait.

While at Little Macatina Harbour, on the coast of Labrador, in July 1833, I saw a Raven's nest placed under the shelvings of the rugged and fearful rocks that form one side of that singular place. The young were nearly fledged, and now and then called loudly to their parents, as if to inquire why our vessel had come there. One of them in attempting to fly away fell into the water. It was secured, when I trimmed one of its wings, and turned it loose on the deck along with some other birds. The mother, however, kept sailing high over

79

the schooner, repeating some notes, which it seems the young one understood, for it walked carefully to the end of the bowsprit, opened its wings, and tried to fly, but being unable, fell into the water and was drowned. In a few days the rest of the family left the place, and we saw no more of them. Some of the sailors who had come to the harbour eight years in succession, assured me that they had always observed the Ravens breeding there. My whole party found it impossible to shoot one of the old ones, who went to the nest and left it with so much caution, that the task of watching them became irksome. One afternoon I concealed myself under a pile of detached rocks for more than two hours. The young frequently croaked as I was waiting there, but no parent came; so I left the place, but the next moment the female was seen from the deck of the Ripley. She alighted in the nest, fed her young, and was off again before I could reach within shooting distance. It was at this place that I observed how singularly well those birds could travel to and from their nest, at a time when I could not, on account of the fog, see them on wing at a greater distance than twenty or thirty yards. On the 29th of the same month, young Ravens were seen in flocks with their parents; but they were already very shy.

GENE STRATTON-PORTER
1863–1924

Born and raised in Wabash County, Indiana, Gene Stratton-Porter spent a restive childhood delighting in nature instead of attending school. At the age of twenty-three, she married a promising pharmacist thirteen years her senior. She settled into the role of homemaker but soon grew restless. Pursuing her lifelong passion for nature, Stratton-Porter began to write about the swamps and wetlands of the Limberlost region of rural Indiana. It was a wise decision: her writings were met with astonishing enthusiasm. Her bestselling novels, children's stories, nature writing and magazine articles earned her a small fortune, enough to found her own Hollywood production company which financed film adaptations of her fiction. She used her celebrity to campaign for the preservation of her beloved Limberlost wetlands. *Moths of the Limberlost* (1916) was the nature book of which she was most proud. In skilful, tender prose, it constructs in meticulous detail an alien world of bursting cocoons, strange exquisite patterns and silent beating wings.

from *Moths of the Limberlost*

In June of 1911, close six o'clock in the evening, I sat on the front veranda of the Cabin, in company with my family, and watched three moths sail past us and around the corner, before I remembered that on the screen of the music-room window to the east there was a solitary female Promethea moth, that day emerged from a cocoon sent me by Professor Rowley. I hurried to the room and found five male moths fluttering before the screen or clinging to the wild grape and sweetbrier vines covering it. I opened the adjoining window and picked up three of the handsomest with my fingers, placing them inside the screen. Then I returned to the veranda. Moths kept coming. We began studying the conditions.

The female had emerged in the dining room on the west side of the cabin. On account of the intense heat of the afternoon sun, that side of the building had been tightly closed all day. At four o'clock the moth was placed on the east window, because it was sheltered with vines. How soon the first male found her, I do not know. There was quite a stiff evening breeze blowing from the west, so that any odour from her would have been carried on east. We sat there and watched and counted six more moths, every one of which came down wind from the west, flying high, above the treetops in fact, and from the direction of a little tree-filled plot called Studabaker's woods. Some of them we could distinguish almost a block away coming straight toward the Cabin, and sailing around the eastern corner with the precision of bounds on a hot trail. How they knew, the Almighty knows; I do not pretend to; but that there was odour distilled by that one female, practically imperceptible to us (she merely smelled like a moth), yet of such strength as to penetrate screen, vines, and roses and reach her kind a block away, *against* considerable breeze, I never shall believe.

[...]

The fact is that moths smell like other moths of the same species, and within a reasonable radius they undoubtedly attract each other. In the same manner birds carry a birdlike odour, and snakes, frogs, fish, bees, and all animals have a scent peculiar to themselves. No dog mistakes the odour of a cat for that of another dog. A cow does not follow the scent of horses to find other cattle. No moth hunts a dragon-fly, a butterfly, or in my experience, even a moth of another species in its search for a mate. How male moths work the miracles I have seen them accomplish in locating females, I cannot explain. As the result of acts we see them perform, we credit some forms of life with much keener scent than others, and many with having the power more highly developed than people. The only standard by which we can determine the effect that the odour of one insect, bird, or animal has upon another is by the effect it has upon us. That a male moth can smell a female a block away, against the wind, when I can detect only a faint musky odour within a foot of her, I do not credit.

Primarily the business of moths is to meet, mate, and deposit eggs that will produce more moths. This is all of life with those that do not take food. That they add the completing touch and most beautiful form of life to a few exquisite May and June nights is their extra good fortune, not any part of the affair of living. With moths that feed and live after reproduction, mating and egg placing comes first. In all cases the rule is much the same. The moths emerge, dry their wings, and reach full development the first day. In freedom, the females being weighted with eggs seldom attempt to fly. They remain where they are, thrust out the egg placer from the last ring of the abdomen and wait. By ten o'clock the males, in such numbers as to amaze a watcher, find them and remain until almost morning. Broad antennæ, slenderer abdomen, and the claspers used in holding the female in mating, smaller wings and more brilliant markings are the signs by which the male can be told in most cases. [...]

A captive moth feels and resents her limitations. I cannot force one to mate even in a large box. I must free her in the conservatory, in a room, or put her on an outside window or door screen. Under these conditions one will place her eggs more nearly as in freedom; but this makes them difficult to find and preserve. Placed in a box and forced by nature to deposit her eggs, as a rule, she will remain in one spot and heap them up until she is forced to move to make room for more. One big female Regalis of the last chapter of this book placed them a thimbleful at a time; but the little caterpillars came rolling out in all directions when due. In my experience, they finish in four or five nights, although I have read of moths having lived and placed eggs for ten, some species being said to have deposited over a thousand. Seven days is usually the limit of life for these big night moths with me: they merely grow inactive and sluggish until the very last, when almost invariably they are seized with a muscular attack, in which they beat themselves to rags and fringes, as if resisting the overcoming lethargy. [...]

At time for emergence the moth bursts the pupa case, which is extremely thin and papery compared with the cases of burrowing species. We know by the wet moth that liquid is ejected, although we cannot see the wet spot on the top of the inner case of Cecropia as we can with Polyphemus, that does not spin the loose outer case and silk nest. From here on the moths emerge according to species. Some work with their mouths and fore feet. Some have rough projections on the top of the head, and others little sawlike arrangements at the bases of the wings. In whatever manner they free themselves, all of them are wet when they leave their quarters. Sometimes the gathered silk ends comb sufficient down from an emerging Cecropia to leave a terra cotta rim around the opening from which it came; but I never saw one lose enough at this time to disfigure it. On very rare occasions a deformed moth appears. I had a Cecropia with one wing no larger than my thumb nail, and it never developed. This is caused by the moth sustaining an injury to the wing in emergence. If the membrane is slightly punctured the liquid forced into the wing for its development escapes and there is no enlargement.

Also, in rare instances, a moth is unable to escape at all and is lost if it is not assisted; but this is precarious business and should not be attempted unless you are positive the moth will die if you do not interfere. The struggle it takes to emerge is a part of the life process of the moth and quickens its circulation and develops its strength for the affairs of life afterward. If the feet have a steady pull to drag forth the body, they will be strong enough to bear its weight while the wings dry and develop.

[...]

As soon as a moth can find a suitable place to cling after it is out, it hangs by the feet and dries the wings and down. Long before it is dry if you try to move a moth or cause disturbance, it will eject several copious jets of a spray from the abdomen that appears, smells and tastes precisely like the liquid found in the abandoned case. If protected from the lightest touch it will do the same. It appeals to me that this liquid is abdominal, partly thrown off to assist the moth in emergence; something very like that bath of birth which accompanies and facilitates human entrance into the

87

world. It helps the struggling moth in separating from the case, wets the down so that it will pass the small opening, reduces the large abdomen so that it will escape the exit, and softens the case and silk where the moth is working. With either male or female the increase in size is so rapid that neither could be returned to their cases five minutes after they have left them.

[...]

Among the moths that do not feed, the year of their evolution is divided into about seven days for the life of the moth, from fifteen to thirty for the eggs, from five to six weeks for the caterpillar and the remainder of the time in the pupa stage. The rule differs with feeding moths only in that after mating and egg placing they take food and live several months, often until quite heavy frosts have fallen.

One can admire to fullest extent the complicated organism, wondrous colouring, and miraculous life processes in the evolution of a moth, but that is all. Their faces express nothing; their attitudes tell no story. There is the marvellous instinct through which the males locate the opposite sex of their species; but one cannot see instinct in the face of any creature; it must develop in acts. There is no part of their lives that makes such pictures of mother-love as birds and animals afford. The male finds a mate and disappears. The female places her eggs and goes out before her caterpillars break their shells. The caterpillar transforms to the moth without its consent, the matter in one upbuilding the other. The entire process is utterly devoid of sentiment, attachment or volition on the part of the creatures involved. They work out a law as inevitable as that which swings suns, moons, and planets in their courses. They are the most fragile and beautiful result of natural law with which I am acquainted.

JEAN-HENRI FABRE
1823–1915

Jean-Henri Fabre, the man Darwin called an 'inimitable observer', was born with the keen eye and hunger for knowledge necessary to succeed in science. An itinerant childhood interrupted his schooling, but Fabre used his spare time to become a formidable autodidact. After teacher training college, he taught at schools and *lycées* around France and authored several popular science books which married his pedagogical skill, his powers of observation and his poetic gifts. After his retirement in 1879, he produced his ten-volume masterpiece, the *Souvenirs entomologiques* (1879–1909), a seminal study of insect life. Written in a riveting and emotive style, the *Souvenirs* made major contributions to our understanding of the insect world. But it is for their deliberately subjective tenor that his writings are included here. Eschewing the bland and neutral tone cultivated by his contemporaries, Fabre favoured a clear emotional involvement with his subjects, going so far as to express horror and even outrage at the unusual mating habits of the captive praying mantis.

'The Mantis.—Courtship'

The little we have seen of the customs of the Mantis does not square very well with the popular name for the insect. From the term *Prégo-Diéu* we should expect a peaceful placid creature, devoutly self-absorbed; and we find a cannibal, a ferocious spectre, biting open the heads of its captives after demoralising them with terror. But we have yet to learn the worst. The customs of the Mantis in connection with its own kin are more atrocious even than those of the spiders, who bear an ill repute in this respect.

To reduce the number of cages on my big laboratory table, to give myself a little more room, while still maintaining a respectable menagerie, I installed several females under one cover. There was sufficient space in the common lodging room for the captives to move about, though for that matter they are not fond of movement, being heavy in the abdomen. Crouching motionless against the wire work of the cover, they will digest their food or await a passing victim. They lived, in short, just as they lived on their native bushes.

Communal life has its dangers. When the hay is low in the manger donkeys grow quarrelsome, although usually so pacific. My guests might well, in a season of dearth, have lost their tempers and begun to fight one another; but I was careful to keep the cages well provided with crickets, which were renewed twice a day. If civil war broke out famine could not be urged in excuse.

At the outset matters did not go badly. The company lived in peace, each Mantis pouncing upon and eating whatever came her way, without interfering with her neighbours. But this period of concord was of brief duration. The bellies of the insects grew fuller: the eggs ripened in their ovaries: the time of courtship and the laying season was approaching. Then a kind of jealous rage seized the females, although no male was present to arouse such feminine rivalry. The swelling of the ovaries perverted my flock, and infected them with an insane desire to devour one another. There were threats, horrid encounters, and cannibal feasts. Once more the spectral pose was seen, the hissing of the wings, and the terrible gesture of the talons outstretched and raised above the head. The females could not have looked more terrible before a grey cricket or a Decticus. Without any motives that I could see, two neighbours suddenly arose in the attitude of conflict. They turned their heads to the right and the left, provoking one another, insulting one another. The *pouf! pouf!* of the wings rubbed by the abdomen sounded the charge. Although the duel was to terminate at the first scratch, without any more serious consequence, the murderous talons, at first folded, open like the leaves of a book, and are extended laterally to protect the long waist and abdomen. The pose is superb, but less terrific than that assumed when the fight is to be to the death.

Then one of the grappling-hooks with a sudden spring flies out and strikes the rival; with the same suddenness it flies back and assumes a position of guard. The adversary replies with a riposte. The fencing reminds one not a little of two cats boxing one another's ears. At the first sign of blood on the soft abdomen, or even at the slightest wound, one admits herself to be conquered and retires. The other refurls her battle standard and goes elsewhere to meditate the capture of a cricket, apparently calm, but in reality ready to recommence the quarrel.

Very often the matter turns out more tragically. In duels to the death the pose of attack is assumed in all its beauty. The murderous talons unfold and rise in the air. Woe to the vanquished! for the victor seizes her in her vice-like grip and at once commences to eat her; beginning, needless to say, at the back of the neck. The odious meal proceeds as calmly as if it were merely a matter of munching a grasshopper; and the survivor enjoys her sister quite as much as lawful game. The spectators do not protest, being only too willing to do the like on the first occasion.

Ferocious creatures! It is said that even wolves do not eat one another. The Mantis is not so scrupulous; she will eat her fellows when her favourite quarry, the cricket, is attainable and abundant.

These observations reach a yet more revolting extreme. Let us inquire into the habits of the insect at breeding time, and to avoid the confusion of a crowd let us isolate the couples under different covers. Thus each pair will have their own dwelling, where nothing can trouble their honeymoon. We will not forget to provide them with abundant food; there shall not be the excuse of hunger for what is to follow.

We are near the end of August. The male Mantis, a slender and elegant lover, judges the time to be propitious. He makes eyes at his powerful companion; he turns his head towards her; he bows his neck and raises his thorax. His little pointed face almost seems to wear an expression. For a long time he stands thus motionless, in contemplation of the desired one. The latter, as though indifferent, does not stir. Yet the lover has seized upon a sign of consent: a sign of which I do not know the secret. He approaches: suddenly he erects his wings, which are shaken with a convulsive tremor.

This is his declaration. He throws himself timidly on the back of his corpulent companion; he clings to her desperately, and steadies himself. The prelude to the embrace is generally lengthy, and the embrace will sometimes last for five or six hours.

Nothing worthy of notice occurs during this time. Finally the two separate, but they are soon to be made one flesh in a much more intimate fashion. If the poor lover is loved by his mistress as the giver of fertility, she also loves him as the choicest of game. During the day, or at latest on the morrow, he is seized by his companion, who first gnaws through the back of his neck, according to use and wont, and then methodically devours him, mouthful by mouthful, leaving only the wings. Here we have no case of jealousy, but simply a depraved taste.

I had the curiosity to wonder how a second male would be received by a newly fecundated female. The result of my inquiry was scandalous. The Mantis in only too many cases is never sated with embraces and conjugal feasts. After a rest, of variable duration, whether the eggs have been laid or not, a second male is welcomed and devoured like the first. A third succeeds him, does his duty, and affords yet another meal. A fourth suffers a like fate. In the course of two weeks I have seen the same Mantis treat seven husbands in this fashion. She admitted all to her embraces, and all paid for the nuptial ecstasy with their lives.

There are exceptions, but such orgies are frequent. On very hot days, when the atmospheric tension is high, they are almost the general rule. At such times the Mantis is all nerves. Under covers which contain large households the females devour one another more frequently than ever; under the covers which contain isolated couples the males are devoured more eagerly than usual when their office has been fulfilled.

I might urge, in mitigation of these conjugal atrocities, that the Mantis does not commit them when at liberty. The male, his function once fulfilled, surely has time to wander off, to escape far away, to flee the terrible spouse, for in my cages he is given a respite, often of a whole day. What really happens by the roadside and in the thickets I do not know; chance, a poor school-mistress, has never instructed me concerning the love-affairs of the Mantis when at liberty. I am obliged to watch events in my laboratory, where the captives, enjoying plenty of sunshine, well nourished, and comfortably lodged, do not seem in any way to suffer from nostalgia. They should behave there as they behave under normal conditions.

Alas! the facts force me to reject the statement that the males have time to escape; for I once surprised a male, apparently in the performance of his vital functions, holding the female tightly embraced—but he had no head, no neck, scarcely any thorax! The female, her head turned over her shoulder, was peacefully browsing on the remains of her lover! And the masculine remnant, firmly anchored, continued its duty!

Love, it is said, is stronger than death! Taken literally, never has an aphorism received a more striking confirmation. Here was a creature decapitated, amputated as far as the middle of the thorax; a corpse which still struggled to give life. It would not relax its hold until the abdomen itself, the seat of the organs of procreation, was attacked.

The custom of eating the lover after the consummation of the nuptials, of making a meal of the exhausted pigmy, who is henceforth good for nothing, is not so difficult to understand, since insects can hardly be accused of sentimentality; but to devour him during the act surpasses anything that the most morbid mind could imagine. I have seen the thing with my own eyes, and I have not yet recovered from my surprise.

Could this unfortunate creature have fled and saved himself, being thus attacked in the performance of his functions? No. We must conclude that the loves of the Mantis are fully as tragic, perhaps even more so, than those of the spider. I do not deny that the limited area of the cage may favour the massacre of the males; but the cause of such butchering must be sought elsewhere. It is perhaps a reminiscence of the carboniferous period when the insect world gradually took shape through prodigious procreation. The Orthoptera, of which the Mantes form a branch, are the firstborn of the insect world.

Uncouth, incomplete in their transformation, they wandered amidst the arborescent foliage, already flourishing when none of the insects sprung of more complex forms of metamorphosis were as yet in existence: neither butterflies, beetles, flies, nor bees. Manners were not gentle in those epochs, which were full of the lust to destroy in order to produce; and the Mantis, a feeble memory of those ancient ghosts, might well preserve the customs of an earlier age. The utilisation of the males as food is a custom in the case of other members of the

Mantis family. It is, I must admit, a general habit. The little grey Mantis, so small and looking so harmless in her cage, which never seeks to harm her neighbours in spite of her crowded quarters, falls upon her male and devours him as ferociously as the Praying Mantis. I have worn myself out in trying to procure the indispensable complements to my female specimens. No sooner is my capture, strongly winged, vigorous and alert, introduced into the cage than he is seized, more often than not, by one of the females who no longer have need of his assistance, and devoured. Once the ovaries are satisfied the two species of Mantis conceive an antipathy for the male; or rather they regard him merely as a particularly tasty species of game.

WANDERING

WILLIAM BARTRAM
1739–1823

An accomplished botanist and natural historian, William Bartram is best remembered as an explorer. His evocative account of his many *Travels Through North & South Carolina, Georgia, East & West Florida, the Cherokee Country, the Extensive Territories of the Muscogulges, or Creek Confederacy, and the Country of the Chactaws* was published in 1791. Referred to simply as *Bartram's Travels*, the work was an instant success, recognized by readers around the world for its scientific contributions and its striking literary qualities. He wrote with lyrical vigour about all things venomous, poisonous, carnivorous and hazardous that he discovered in the swamplands and forests of the Southern United States, such as, in the following passages, the American alligator. His *Travels* are also remarkable for their sympathetic portrayal of Native Americans, unusual in the literature of his time.

from *Travels Through North & South Carolina*

The evening was temperately cool and calm. The crocodiles began to roar and appear in uncommon numbers along the shores and in the river. I fixed my camp in an open plain, near the utmost projection of the promontory, under the shelter of a large live oak, which stood on the highest part of the ground, and but a few yards from my boat. From this open, high situation, I had a free prospect of the river, which was a matter of no trivial consideration to me, having good reason to dread the subtle attacks of the alligators, who were crowding about my harbour. Having collected a good quantity of wood for the purpose of keeping up a light and smoke during the night, I began to think of preparing my supper, when, upon examining my stores, I found but a scanty provision. I thereupon determined, as the most expeditious way of supplying my necessities, to take my bob and try for some trout. About one hundred yards above my harbour began a cove or bay of the river, out of which opened a large lagoon. The mouth or entrance from the river to it was narrow, but the waters soon after spread and formed a little lake, extending into the marshes: its entrance and shores within I observed to be verged with floating lawns of the pistia and nymphea and other aquatic plants; these I knew were excellent haunts for trout.

The verges and islets of the lagoon were elegantly embellished with flowering plants and shrubs; the laughing coots with wings half spread were tripping over the little coves, and hiding themselves in the tufts of grass; young broods of the painted summer teal, skimming the still surface of the waters, and following the watchful parent unconscious of danger, were frequently surprised by the voracious trout; and he, in turn, as often by the subtle greedy alligator. Behold him rushing forth from the flags and reeds. His enormous body swells. His plaited tail brandished high, floats upon the lake. The waters like a cataract descend from his opening jaws. Clouds of smoke issue from his dilated nostrils. The earth trembles with his thunder. When immediately from the opposite coast of the lagoon, emerges from the deep his rival champion. They suddenly dart upon each other. The boiling surface of the lake marks their rapid course, and a terrific conflict commences. They now sink to the bottom folded together in horrid wreaths. The water becomes thick and discoloured. Again they rise, their jaws clap together, re-echoing through the deep surrounding forests. Again they sink, when the contest ends at the muddy bottom of the lake, and the vanquished makes a hazardous escape, hiding himself in the muddy turbulent waters and sedge on a distant shore. The proud victor exulting returns to the place of action. The shores and forests resound his dreadful roar, together with the triumphing shouts of the plaited tribes around, witnesses of the horrid combat.

My apprehensions were highly alarmed after being a spectator of so dreadful a battle. It was obvious that every delay would but tend to increase my dangers and difficulties, as the sun was near setting, and the alligators gathered around my harbour from all quarters. From these considerations I concluded to be expeditious in my trip to the lagoon, in order to take some fish. Not thinking it prudent to take my fusee with me, lest I might lose it overboard in case of a battle, which I had every reason to dread before my return, I therefore furnished myself with a club for my defence, went on board, and penetrating the first line of those which surrounded my harbour, they gave way; but being pursued by several very large ones, I kept strictly on the watch, and paddled with all my might towards the entrance of the lagoon, hoping to be sheltered there from the multitude of my assailants; but ere I had half-way reached the place, I was attacked on all sides, several endeavouring to overset the canoe. My situation now became precarious to the last degree: two very large ones attacked me closely, at the same instant, rushing up with their heads and part of their bodies above the water, roaring terribly and belching floods of water over me. They struck their jaws together so close to my ears, as almost to stun me, and I expected every moment to be dragged out of the boat and instantly devoured. But I applied my weapons so effectually about me, though at random, that I was so successful as to beat them off a little; when, finding that they designed to renew the battle, I made for the shore, as the only means left me for my preservation; for, by keeping close to it, I should have my enemies on one side of me only, whereas I was before surrounded by them; and there was a probability, if pushed to the last extremity, of saving myself, by jumping out of the canoe on shore, as it is easy to outwalk them on land, although comparatively as swift as lightning in the water. I found this last expedient alone could fully answer my expectations, for as soon as I gained the shore, they drew off and kept aloof. This was a happy relief, as my confidence was, in some degree, recovered by it. On recollecting myself, I discovered that I had almost reached the entrance of the lagoon, and determined to venture in, if possible, to take a few fish, and then return to my harbour, while day-light continued; for I could now, with caution and resolution, make my way with safety along shore; and indeed there was no other way to regain my camp, without leaving my boat and making my retreat through the marshes and reeds, which, if I could even effect, would have been in a manner throwing myself away, for then there would have been no hopes of ever recovering my bark, and returning in safety to any settlements of men. I accordingly proceeded, and made good my entrance into the lagoon, though not without opposition from the alligators, who formed a line across the entrance, but did not pursue me into it, nor was I molested by any there, though there were some very large ones in a cove at the upper end. I soon caught more trout than I had present occasion for, and the air was too hot and sultry to admit of their being kept for many hours, even though salted or barbecued. I now prepared for my return to camp, which I succeeded in with but little trouble, by keeping close to the shore; yet I was opposed upon re-entering the river out of the lagoon, and pursued near to my landing (though not closely attacked), particularly by an old daring one, about twelve feet in length, who kept close after me; and when I stepped on shore and turned about, in order to draw up my canoe, he rushed up near my feet, and lay there for some time, looking me in the face, his head and shoulders out of water. I resolved he should pay for his temerity, and having a heavy load in my fusee, I ran to my camp, and returning with my piece, found him with his foot on the gunwale of the boat, in search of fish. On my coming up he withdrew sullenly and slowly into the water, but soon returned and placed himself in his former position, looking at me, and seeming neither fearful nor any way disturbed. I soon dispatched him by lodging the contents of my gun in his head, and then proceeded to cleanse and prepare my fish for supper; and accordingly took them out of the boat, laid them down on the sand close to the water, and began to scale them; when, raising my head, I saw before me, through the clear water, the head and shoulders of a very large alligator, moving slowly towards me. I instantly stepped back, when, with a sweep of his tail, he brushed off several of my fish. It was certainly most providential that I looked up at that instant, as the monster would probably, in less than a minute, have seized and dragged me into the river. This incredible boldness of the

109

animal disturbed me greatly, supposing there could now be no reasonable safety for me during the night, but by keeping continually on the watch: I therefore, as soon as I had prepared the fish, proceeded to secure myself and effects in the best manner I could. In the first place, I hauled my bark upon the shore, almost clear out of the water, to prevent their over-setting or sinking her; after this, every moveable was taken out and carried to my camp, which was but a few yards off; then ranging some dry wood in such order as was the most convenient, I cleared the ground round about it, that there might be no impediment in my way, in case of an attack in the night, either from the water or the land; for I discovered by this time, that this small isthmus, from its remote situation and fruitfulness, was resorted to by bears and wolves. Having prepared myself in the best manner I could, I charged my gun, and proceeded to reconnoitre my camp and the adjacent grounds; when I discovered that the peninsula and grove, at the distance of about two hundred yards from my encampment, on the land side, were invested by a cypress swamp, covered with water, which below was joined to the shore of the little lake, and above to the marshes surrounding the lagoon; so that I was confined to an islet exceedingly circumscribed, and I found there was no other retreat for me, in case of an attack, but by either ascending one of the large oaks, or pushing off with my boat.

It was by this time dusk, and the alligators had nearly ceased their roar, when I was again alarmed by a tumultuous noise that seemed to be in my harbour, and therefore engaged my immediate attention. Returning to my camp, I found it undisturbed, and then continued on to the extreme point of the promontory, where I saw a scene, new and surprising, which at first threw my senses into such a tumult, that it was some time before I could comprehend what was the matter; however, I soon accounted for the prodigious assemblage of crocodiles at this place, which exceeded every thing of the kind I had ever heard of.

How shall I express myself so as to convey an adequate idea of it to the reader, and at the same time avoid raising suspicions of my veracity? Should I say, that the river (in this place) from shore to shore, and perhaps near half a mile above and below me, appeared to be one solid bank of fish, of various kinds, pushing through this narrow pass of St. Juan's into the little lake, on their return down the river, and that the alligators were in such incredible numbers, and so close together from shore to shore, that it would have been easy to have walked across on their heads, had the animals been harmless? What expressions can sufficiently declare the shocking scene that for some minutes continued, whilst this mighty army of fish were forcing the pass? During this attempt, thousands, I may say hundreds of thousands, of them were caught and swallowed by the devouring alligators. I have seen an alligator take up out of the water several great fish at a time, and just squeeze them betwixt his jaws, while the tails of the great trout flapped about his eyes and lips, ere he had swallowed them. The horrid noise of their closing jaws, their plunging amidst the broken banks of fish, and rising with their prey some feet upright above the water, the floods of water and blood rushing out of their mouths, and the clouds of vapour issuing from their wide nostrils, were truly frightful. This scene continued at intervals during the night, as the fish came to the pass. After this sight, shocking and tremendous as it was, I found myself somewhat easier and more reconciled to my situation; being convinced that their extraordinary assemblage here was owing to the annual feast of fish; and that they were so well employed in their own element, that I had little occasion to fear their paying me a visit.

It being now almost night, I returned to my camp, where I had left my fish broiling, and my kettle of rice stewing; and having with me oil, pepper, and salt, and excellent oranges hanging in abundance over my head (a valuable substitute for vinegar) I sat down and regaled myself cheerfully. Having finished my repast, I rekindled my fire for light, and whilst I was revising the notes of my past day's journey, I was suddenly roused with a noise behind me toward the main land. I sprang up on my feet, and listening, I distinctly heard some creature wading the water of the isthmus. I seized my gun and went cautiously from my camp, directing my steps towards the noise: when I had advanced about thirty yards, I halted behind a coppice of orange trees, and soon perceived two very large bears, which had made their way through the water, and had landed in the grove, about one hundred yards distance from me, and were advancing towards me. I waited until they were within thirty yards of me: they there began to snuff and look towards my camp: I snapped my piece, but it flashed, on which they both turned about and galloped off, plunging through the water and swamp, never halting, as I suppose, until they reached fast land, as I could hear them leaping and plunging a long time. They did not presume to return again, nor was I molested by any other creature, except being occasionally awakened by the whooping of owls, screaming of bitterns, or the wood-rats running amongst the leaves.

The wood-rat is a very curious animal. It is not half the size of the domestic rat; of a dark brown or black colour; its tail slender and shorter in proportion, and covered thinly with short hair. It is singular with respect to its ingenuity and great labour in the construction of its habitation, which is a conical pyramid about three or four feet high, constructed with dry branches, which it collects with great labour and perseverance, and piles up without any apparent order; yet they are so interwoven with one another, that it would take a bear or wild-cat some time to pull one of these castles to pieces, and allow the animals sufficient time to secure a retreat with their young.

The noise of the crocodiles kept me awake the greater part of the night; but when I arose in the morning, contrary to my expectations, there was perfect peace; very few of them to be seen, and those were asleep on the shore. Yet I was not able to suppress my fears and apprehensions of being attacked by them in future; and indeed yesterday's combat with them, notwithstanding I came off in a manner victorious, or at least made a safe retreat, had left sufficient impression on my mind to damp my courage; and it seemed too much for one of my strength, being alone in a very small boat, to encounter such collected danger. To pursue my voyage up the river, and be obliged every evening to pass such dangerous defiles, appeared to me as perilous as running the gauntlet betwixt two rows of Indians armed with knives and firebrands. I however resolved to continue my voyage one day longer, if I possibly could with safety, and then return down the river, should I find the like difficulties to oppose. Accordingly I got every thing on board, charged my gun, and set sail, cautiously, along shore. As I passed by Battle lagoon, I began to tremble and keep a good look-out; when suddenly a huge alligator rushed out of the reeds, and with a tremendous roar came up, and darted as swift as an arrow under my boat, emerging upright on my lee quarter, with open jaws, and belching water and smoke that fell upon me like rain in a hurricane. I laid soundly about his head with my club, and beat him off; and after plunging and darting about my boat, he went off on a straight line through the water, seemingly with the rapidity of lightning, and entered the cape of the lagoon. I now employed my time to the very best advantage in paddling close along shore, but could not forbear looking now and then behind me, and presently perceived one of them coming up again. The water of the river hereabouts was shoal and very clear; the monster came up with the usual roar and menaces, and passed close by the side of my boat, when I could distinctly see a young brood of alligators, to the number of one hundred or more, following after her in a long train. They kept close together in a column, without straggling off to the one side or the other; the young appeared to be of an equal size, about fifteen inches in length, almost black, with pale yellow transverse waved clouds or blotches, much like rattlesnakes in colour. I now lost sight of my enemy again.

Still keeping close along shore, on turning a point or projection of the river bank, at once I beheld a great number of hillocks or small pyramids, resembling hay-cocks, ranged like an encampment along the banks. They stood fifteen or twenty yards distant from the water, on a high marsh, about four feet perpendicular above the water. I knew them to be the nests of the crocodile, having had a description of them before; and now expected a furious and general attack, as I saw several large crocodiles swimming abreast of these buildings. These nests being so great a curiosity to me, I was determined at all events immediately to land and examine them. Accordingly, I ran my bark on shore at one of their landing-places, which was a sort of nick or little dock, from which ascended a sloping path or road up to the edge of the meadow, where their nests were; most of them were deserted, and the great thick whitish egg-shells lay broken and scattered upon the ground round about them.

The nests or hillocks are of the form of an obtuse cone, four feet high and four or five feet in diameter at their bases; they are constructed with mud, grass and herbage. At first they lay a floor of this kind of tempered mortar on the ground, upon which they deposit a layer of eggs, and upon this a stratum of mortar, seven or eight inches in thickness, and then another layer of eggs; and in this manner one stratum upon another, nearly to the top. I believe they commonly lay from one to two hundred eggs in a nest: these are hatched, I suppose, by the heat of the sun; and perhaps the vegetable substances mixed with the earth, being acted upon by the sun, may cause a small degree of fermentation, and so increase the heat in those hillocks. The ground for several acres about these nests shewed evident marks of a continual resort of alligators; the grass was every where beaten down, hardly a blade or straw was left standing; whereas, all about, at a distance, it was five or six feet high, and as thick as it could grow together.

The female, as I imagine, carefully watches her own nest of eggs until they are all hatched; or perhaps while she is attending her own brood, she takes under her care and protection as many as she can get at one time, either from her own particular nest or others; but certain it is, that the young are not left to shift for themselves; for I have had frequent opportunities of seeing the female alligator leading about the shores her train of young ones, just as a hen does her brood of chickens; and she is equally assiduous and courageous in defending the young, which are under her care, and providing for their subsistence; and when she is basking upon the warm banks, with her brood around her, you may hear the young ones continually whining and barking like young puppies. I believe but few of a brood live to the years of full growth and magnitude, as the old feed on the young as long as they can make prey of them.

The alligator when full grown is a very large and terrible creature, and of prodigious strength, activity and swiftness in the water. I have seen them twenty feet in length, and some are supposed to be twenty-two or twenty-three feet. Their body is as large as that of a horse; their shape exactly resembles that of a lizard, except their tail, which is flat or cuneiform, being compressed on each side, and gradually diminishing from the abdomen to the extremity, which, with the whole body is covered with horny plates or squammæ, impenetrable when on the body of the live animal, even to a rifle ball, except about their head and just behind their fore-legs or arms, where it is said they are only vulnerable. The head of a full grown one is about three feet, and the mouth opens nearly the same length; their eyes are small in proportion, and seem sunk deep in the head, by means of the prominency of the brows; the nostrils are large, inflated and prominent on the top, so that the head in the water resembles, at a distance, a great chunk of wood floating about. Only the upper jaw moves, which they raise almost perpendicular, so as to form a right angle with the lower one. In the forepart of the upper jaw, on each side, just under the nostrils, are two very large, thick, strong teeth or tusks, not very sharp, but rather the shape of a cone: these are as white as the finest polished ivory, and are not covered by any skin or lips, and always in sight, which gives the creature a frightful appearance: in the lower jaw are holes opposite to these teeth, to receive them: when they clap their jaws together it causes a surprising noise, like that which is made by forcing a heavy plank with violence upon the ground, and may be heard at a great distance.

But what is yet more surprising to a stranger, is the incredible loud and terrifying roar, which they are capable of making, especially in the spring season, their breeding time. It most resembles very heavy distant thunder, not only shaking the air and waters, but causing the earth to tremble; and when hundreds and thousands are roaring at the same time, you can scarcely be persuaded, but that the whole globe is violently and dangerously agitated.

An old champion, who is perhaps absolute sovereign of a little lake or lagoon (when fifty less than himself are obliged to content themselves with swelling and roaring in little coves round about) darts forth from the reedy coverts all at once, on the surface of the waters, in a right line; at first seemingly as rapid as lightning, but gradually more slowly until he arrives at the centre of the lake, when he stops. He now swells himself by drawing in wind and water through his mouth, which causes a loud sonorous rattling in the throat for near a minute, but it is immediately forced out again through his mouth and nostrils, with a loud noise, brandishing his tail in the air, and the vapour ascending from his nostrils like smoke. At other times, when swollen to an extent ready to burst, his head and tail lifted up, he spins or twirls round on the surface of the water. He acts his part like an Indian chief when rehearsing his feats of war; and then retiring, the exhibition is continued by others who dare to step forth, and strive to excel each other, to gain the attention of the favourite female.

Having gratified my curiosity at this general breeding-place and nursery of crocodiles, I continued my voyage up the river without being greatly disturbed by them.

ROBERT LOUIS STEVENSON
1850–1894

Born in Edinburgh, Scotland, into a family of engineers, the young Robert Louis Stevenson was a frail, eccentric child who struggled to make friends. He suffered chronic respiratory problems which, in early life, led to extended stays in France and, later, to voyages in the Pacific, where he eventually settled, in Samoa, in 1889. Celebrated in his lifetime, Stevenson established his reputation as a gifted storyteller through adventure novels like *Treasure Island* (1881–2) and *Kidnapped* (1886) and with Gothic tales such as *The Strange Case of Dr Jekyll and Mr Hyde* (1886). Stevenson was also an essayist, critic, English and Scots poet and successful travel writer. His now classic *Travels with a Donkey in the Cévennes* (1879) pioneered the genre of so-called outdoor literature. Since publication, countless writers and readers have retraced Stevenson's journey astride his wily obstinate donkey, Modestine, through the craggy and barren Cévennes region of south-central France.

from *Travels With a Donkey in the Cevennes*

From *Bleymard* after dinner, although it was already late, I set out to scale a portion of the *Lozère*. An ill-marked stony drove road guided me forward; and I met nearly half a dozen bullock-carts descending from the woods, each laden with a whole pine-tree for the winter's firing. At the top of the woods, which do not climb very high upon this cold ridge, I struck leftward by a path among the pines, until I hit on a dell of green turf, where a streamlet made a little spout over some stones to serve me for a water-tap. 'In a more sacred or sequestered bower . . . nor nymph, nor faunus, haunted.' The trees were not old, but they grew thickly round the glade: there was no outlook, except north-eastward upon distant hill-tops, or straight upward to the sky; and the encampment felt secure and private like a room. By the time I had made my arrangements and fed *Modestine*, the day was already beginning to decline. I buckled myself to the knees into my sack and made a hearty meal; and as soon as the sun went down, I pulled my cap over my eyes and fell asleep.

Night is a dead monotonous period under a roof; but in the open world it passes lightly, with its stars and dews and perfumes, and the hours are marked by changes in the face of Nature. What seems a kind of temporal death to people choked between walls and curtains, is only a light and living slumber to the man who sleeps a-field. All night long he can hear Nature breathing deeply and freely; even as she takes her rest, she turns and smiles; and there is one stirring hour unknown to those who dwell in houses, when a wakeful influence goes abroad over the sleeping hemisphere, and all the outdoor world are on their feet. It is then that the cock first crows, not this time to announce the dawn, but like a cheerful watchman speeding the course of night. Cattle awake on the meadows; sheep break their fast on dewy hillsides, and change to a new lair among the ferns; and houseless men, who have lain down with the fowls, open their dim eyes and behold the beauty of the night.

At what inaudible summons, at what gentle touch of Nature, are all these sleepers thus recalled in the same hour to life? Do the stars rain down an influence, or do we share some thrill of mother earth below our resting bodies? Even shepherds and old country-folk, who are the deepest read in these arcana, have not a guess as to the means or purpose of this nightly resurrection. Towards two in the morning they declare the thing takes place;

and neither know nor inquire further. And at least it is a pleasant incident. We are disturbed in our slumber only, like the luxurious *Montaigne*, 'that we may the better and more sensibly relish it.' We have a moment to look upon the stars. And there is a special pleasure for some minds in the reflection that we share the impulse with all outdoor creatures in our neighbourhood, that we have escaped out of the *Bastille* of civilisation, and are become, for the time being, a mere kindly animal and a sheep of Nature's flock.

When that hour came to me among the pines, I wakened thirsty. My tin was standing by me half full of water. I emptied it at a draught; and feeling broad awake after this internal cold aspersion, sat upright to make a cigarette. The stars were clear, coloured, and jewel-like, but not frosty. A faint silvery vapour stood for the *Milky Way*. All around me the black fir-points stood upright and stockstill. By the whiteness of the pack-saddle, I could see *Modestine* walking round and round at the length of her tether; I could hear her steadily munching at the sward; but there was not another sound, save the indescribable quiet talk of the runnel over the stones. I lay lazily smoking and studying the colour of the sky, as we call the void of space, from where it showed a reddish gray behind the pines to where it showed a glossy blue-black between the stars. As if to be more like a pedlar, I wear a silver ring. This I could see faintly shining as I raised or lowered the cigarette; and at each whiff the inside of my hand was illuminated, and became for a second the highest light in the landscape.

A faint wind, more like a moving coolness than a stream of air, passed down the glade from time to time; so that even in my great chamber the air was being renewed all night long. I thought with horror of the inn at *Chasseradès* and the congregated nightcaps; with horror of the nocturnal prowesses of clerks and students, of hot theatres and pass-keys and close rooms. I have not often enjoyed a more serene possession of myself, nor felt more independent of material aids. The outer world, from which we cower into our houses, seemed after all a gentle habitable place; and night after night a man's bed, it seemed, was laid and waiting for him in the fields, where God keeps an open house. I thought I had rediscovered one of those truths which are revealed to savages and hid from political economists: at the least, I had discovered a new pleasure for myself. And yet even while I was exulting in my solitude I became aware of a strange lack. I wished a companion to lie near me in the starlight, silent and not moving, but ever within touch. For there is a fellowship more quiet even than solitude, and which, rightly understood, is solitude made perfect. And to live out of doors with the woman a man loves is of all lives the most complete and free.

As I thus lay, between content and longing, a faint noise stole towards me through the pines. I thought, at first, it was the crowing of cocks or the barking of dogs at some very distant farm; but steadily and gradually it took articulate shape in my ears, until I became aware that a passenger was going by upon the high-road in the valley, and singing loudly as he went. There was more of good-will than grace in his performance; but he trolled with ample lungs; and the sound of his voice took hold upon the hillside and set the air shaking in the leafy glens. I have heard people passing by night in sleeping cities; some of them sang; one, I remember, played loudly on the bag-pipes. I have heard the rattle of a cart or carriage spring up suddenly after hours of stillness, and pass, for some minutes, within the range of my hearing as I lay abed. There is a romance about all who are abroad in the black hours, and with something of a thrill we try to guess their business. But here the romance was double: first, this glad passenger, lit internally with wine, who sent up his voice in music through the night; and then I, on the other hand, buckled into my sack, and smoking alone in the pine-woods between four and five thousand feet towards the stars.

When I awoke again (*Sunday, 29th September*), many of the stars had disappeared; only the stronger companions of the night still burned visibly overhead; and away towards the east I saw a faint haze of light upon the horizon, such as had been the *Milky Way* when I was last awake. Day was at hand. I lit my lantern, and by its glowworm light put on my boots and gaiters; then I broke up some bread for *Modestine*, filled my can at the water-tap, and lit my spirit-lamp to boil myself some chocolate. The blue darkness lay long in the glade where I had so sweetly slumbered; but soon there was a broad streak of orange melting into gold along the mountain-tops of *Vivarais*. A solemn glee possessed my mind at this gradual and lovely coming in of day. I heard the runnel with delight; I looked round me for something beautiful and unexpected; but the still black pine-trees, the hollow glade, the munching ass, remained unchanged in figure. Nothing had altered but the light, and that, indeed, shed over all a spirit of life and of breathing peace, and moved me to a strange exhilaration.

I drank my water chocolate, which was hot if it was not rich, and strolled here and there, and up and down about the glade. While I was thus delaying, a gush of steady wind, as long as a heavy sigh, poured direct out of the quarter of the morning. It was cold, and set me sneezing. The trees near at hand tossed their black plumes in its passage; and I could see the thin distant spires of pine along the edge of the hill rock slightly to and fro against the golden east. Ten minutes after, the sunlight spread at a gallop along the hillside, scattering shadows and sparkles, and the day had come completely.

I hastened to prepare my pack, and tackle the steep ascent that lay before me; but I had something on my mind. It was only a fancy; yet a fancy will sometimes be importunate. I had been most hospitably received and punctually served in my green caravanserai. The room was airy, the water excellent, and the dawn had called me to a moment. I say nothing of the tapestries or the inimitable ceiling, nor yet of the view which I commanded from the windows; but I felt I was in some one's debt for all this liberal entertainment. And so it pleased me, in a half-laughing way, to leave pieces of money on the turf as I went along, until I had left enough for my night's lodging. I trust they did not fall to some rich and churlish drover.

HENRY DAVID THOREAU
1817–1862

In Concord, Massachusetts, where he was born and died, Henry David Thoreau wrote poetry and lectured, studied botany and moral philosophy, campaigned for the abolition of slavery, lived as a vegetarian and pioneered the notion of civil disobedience, an idea which went on to influence Mahatma Gandhi and Martin Luther King Jr. If this wasn't enough for one short life, Thoreau also worked at various times as a repairman and gardener, editor and tutor, as a schoolteacher, surveyor and pencil-maker. He is best known, however, for his unorthodox memoir *Walden* (1854). In spectacular prose, Thoreau describes his attempt to live in harmony with the environment at the edge of Concord around Walden Pond. Thoreau's writings and way of life played a significant role in inspiring modern environmentalism, and he has had a lasting impact on the way we conceive our place in nature. His essay 'Walking' (1862) sets out in characteristically pugnacious style some of his key positions on the preservation and appreciation of the natural world.

130

from 'Walking'

I wish to speak a word for Nature, for absolute freedom and wildness, as contrasted with a freedom and culture merely civil,—to regard man as an inhabitant, or a part and parcel of Nature, rather than a member of society. I wish to make an extreme statement, if so I may make an emphatic one, for there are enough champions of civilization: the minister, and the school-committee, and every one of you will take care of that.

[...]

[W]hat I have been preparing to say is, that in Wildness is the preservation of the world. Every tree sends its fibres forth in search of the Wild. The cities import it at any price. Men plough and sail for it. From the forest and wilderness come the tonics and barks which brace mankind. Our ancestors were savages. The story of Romulus and Remus being suckled by a wolf is not a meaningless fable. The founders of every State which has risen to eminence have drawn their nourishment and vigor from a similar wild source. It was because the children of the Empire were not suckled by the wolf that they were conquered and displaced by the children of the Northern forests who were.

I believe in the forest, and in the meadow, and in the night in which the corn grows. We require an infusion of hem-lock-spruce or arbor-vitæ in our tea. There is a difference between eating and drinking for strength and from mere gluttony. The Hottentots eagerly devour the marrow of the koodoo and other antelopes raw, as a matter of course. Some of our Northern Indians eat raw the marrow of the Arctic reindeer, as well as various other parts, including the summits of the antlers, as long as they are soft. And herein, perchance, they have stolen a march on the cooks of Paris. They get what usually goes to feed the fire. This is probably better than stall-fed beef and slaughter-house pork to make a man of. Give me a wildness whose glance no civilization can endure,—as if we lived on the marrow of koodoos devoured raw.

There are some intervals which border the strain of the wood-thrush, to which I would migrate,—wild lands where no settler has squatted; to which, methinks, I am already acclimated.

The African hunter Cummings tells us that the skin of the eland, as well as that of most other antelopes just killed, emits the most delicious perfume of trees and grass. I would have every man so much like a wild antelope, so much a part and parcel of Nature, that his very person should thus sweetly advertise our senses of his presence, and remind us of those parts of Nature which he most haunts. I feel no disposition to be satirical, when the trapper's coat emits the odor of musquash even; it is a sweeter scent to me than that which commonly exhales from the merchant's or the scholar's garments. When I go into their wardrobes and handle their vestments, I am reminded of no grassy plains and flowery meads which they have frequented, but of dusty merchants' exchanges and libraries rather.

A tanned skin is something more than respectable, and perhaps olive is a fitter color than white for a man,—a denizen of the woods. "The pale white man!" I do not wonder that the African pitied him. Darwin the naturalist says, "A white man bathing by the side of a Tahitian was like a plant bleached by the gardener's art, compared with a fine, dark green one, growing vigorously in the open fields."

Ben Jonson exclaims,—

      "How near to good is what is fair!"

So I would say,—

      How near to good is what is *wild!*

Life consists with wildness. The most alive is the wildest. Not yet subdued to man, its presence refreshes him. One who pressed forward incessantly and never rested from his labors, who grew fast and made infinite demands on life, would always find himself in a new country or wilderness, and surrounded by the raw material of life. He would be climbing over the prostrate stems of primitive forest-trees.

Hope and the future for me are not in lawns and cultivated fields, not in towns and cities, but in the impervious and quaking swamps. When, formerly, I have analyzed my partiality for some farm which I had contemplated purchasing, I have frequently found that I was attracted solely by a few square rods of impermeable and unfathomable bog,—a natural sink in one corner of it. That was the jewel which dazzled me. I derive more of my subsistence from the swamps which surround my native town than from the cultivated gardens in the village. There are no richer parterres to my eyes than the dense beds of dwarf andromeda (*Cassandra calyculata*) which cover these tender places on the earth's surface. Botany cannot go farther than tell me the names of the shrubs which grow there,— the high-blueberry, panicled andromeda, lamb-kill, azalea, and rhodora,—all standing in the quaking sphagnum. I often think that I should like to have my house front on this mass of dull red bushes, omitting other flower plots and borders, transplanted spruce and trim box, even gravelled walks,—to have this fertile spot under my windows, not a few imported barrow-fulls of soil only to cover the sand which was thrown out in digging the cellar. Why not put my house, my parlor, behind this plot, instead of behind that meagre assemblage of curiosities, that poor apology for a Nature and Art, which I call my front-yard? It is an effort to clear up and make a decent appearance when the carpenter and mason have departed, though done as much for the passer-by as the dweller within. The most tasteful front-yard fence was never an agreeable object of study to me; the most elaborate ornaments, acorn-tops, or what not, soon wearied and disgusted me. Bring your sills up to the very edge of the swamp, then, (though it may not be the best place for a dry cellar,) so that there be no access on that side to citizens. Front-yards are not made to walk in, but, at most, through, and you could go in the back way.

Yes, though you may think me perverse, if it were proposed to me to dwell in the neighborhood of the most beautiful garden that ever human art contrived, or else of a dismal swamp, I should certainly decide for the swamp. How vain, then, have been all your labors, citizens, for me!

My spirits infallibly rise in proportion to the outward dreariness. Give me the ocean, the desert, or the wilderness! In the desert, pure air and solitude compensate for want of moisture and fertility. The traveller Burton says of it,—"Your *morale* improves; you become frank and cordial, hospitable and single-minded . . . . In the desert, spirituous liquors excite only disgust. There is a keen enjoyment in a mere animal existence." They who have been travelling long on the steppes of Tartary say,—"On reëntering cultivated lands, the agitation, perplexity, and turmoil of civilization oppressed and suffocated us; the air seemed to fail us, and we felt every moment as if about to die of asphyxia." When I would recreate myself, I seek the darkest wood, the thickest and most interminable, and, to the citizen, most dismal swamp. I enter a swamp as a sacred place,—a *sanctum sanctorum.* There is the strength, the marrow of Nature. The wild-wood covers the virgin mould,—and the same soil is good for men and for trees. A man's health requires as many acres of meadow to his prospect as his farm does loads of muck. There are the strong meats on which he feeds. A town is saved, not more by the righteous men in it than by the woods and swamps that surround it. A township where one primitive forest waves above, while another primitive forest rots below,—such a town is fitted to raise not only corn and potatoes, but poets and philosophers for the coming ages. In such a soil grew Homer and Confucius and the rest, and out of such a wilderness comes the Reformer eating locusts and wild honey.

To preserve wild animals implies generally the creation of a forest for them to dwell in or resort to. So is it with man. A hundred years ago they sold bark in our streets peeled from our own woods. In the very aspect of those primitive and rugged trees, there was, methinks, a tanning principle which hardened and consolidated the fibres of men's thoughts. Ah! already I shudder for these comparatively degenerate days of my native village, when you cannot collect a load of bark of good thickness,—and we no longer produce tar and turpentine.

[...]

In short, all good things are wild and free. There is something in a strain of music, whether produced by an instrument or by the human voice,—take the sound of a bugle in a summer night, for instance,—which by its wildness, to speak without satire, reminds me of the cries emitted by wild beasts in their native forests. It is so much of their wildness as I can understand. Give me for my friends and neighbors wild men, not tame ones. The wildness of the savage is but a faint symbol of the awful ferity with which good men and lovers meet.

I love even to see the domestic animals reassert their native rights,—any evidence that they have not wholly lost their original wild habits and vigor; as when my neighbor's cow breaks out of her pasture early in the spring and boldly swims the river, a cold, gray tide, twenty-five or thirty rods wide, swollen by the melted snow. It is the buffalo crossing the Mississippi. This exploit confers some dignity on the herd in my eyes,—already dignified. The seeds of instinct are preserved under the thick hides of cattle and horses, like seeds in the bowels of the earth, an indefinite period.

Any sportiveness in cattle is unexpected. I saw one day a herd of a dozen bullocks and cows running about and frisking in unwieldy sport, like huge rats, even like kittens. They shook their heads, raised their tails, and rushed up and down a hill, and I perceived by their horns, as well as by their activity, their relation to the deer tribe. But, alas! a sudden loud *Whoa!* would have damped their ardor at once, reduced them from venison to beef, and stiffened their sides and sinews like the locomotive. Who but the Evil One has cried, "Whoa!" to mankind? Indeed, the life of cattle, like that of many men, is but a sort of locomotiveness; they move a side at a time, and man, by his machinery, is meeting the horse and ox half-way. Whatever part the whip has touched is thenceforth palsied. Who would ever think of a *side* of any of the supple cat tribe, as we speak of a *side* of beef?

I rejoice that horses and steers have to be broken before they can be made the slaves of men, and that men themselves have some wild oats still left to sow before they become submissive members of society. Undoubtedly, all men are not equally fit subjects for civilization; and because the majority, like dogs and sheep, are tame by inherited disposition, this is no reason why the others should have their natures broken that they may be reduced to the same level. Men are in the main alike, but they were made several in order that they might be various. If a low use is to be served, one man will do nearly or quite as well as another; if a high one, individual excellence is to be regarded. Any man can stop a hole to keep the wind away, but no other man could serve so rare a use as the author of this illustration did. Confucius says,—"The skins of the tiger and the leopard, when they are tanned, are as the skins of the dog and the sheep tanned." But it is not the part of a true culture to tame tigers, any more than it is to make sheep ferocious; and tanning their skins for shoes is not the best use to which they can be put.

CONTEMPLATION

SEI SHŌNAGON
c. 966–1017 / 1025

At the end of the tenth century, Sei Shōnagon
served as lady-in-waiting to the Empress Teishi,
consort to the Emperor Ichijō, at the Imperial
Court in Kyoto. Lady Sei, as she is often known,
occupied a relatively low position in the court hier-
archy, and she might have disappeared to history
were it not for two remarkable literary events.
First, her rivalry with Murasaki Shikibu, another
court lady and author of *The Tale of Genji* (*c.* 1008),
a classic of Japanese literature often described as
the world's first novel. Second, the creation of
Lady Sei's own literary classic, *The Pillow Book*, a
collection of poems, anecdotes, essays and observations. Written in a lithe, evocative style, *The
Pillow Book* is illuminated by Sei Shōnagon's ironic
wit and super-subtle sensibility as she ponders and
describes everyday life in Heian-period Japan,
from customs at court to the exquisite melancholy
of the changing seasons.

from *The Pillow Book of Sei Shōnagon*

In spring it is the dawn that is most beautiful. As the light creeps over the hills, their outlines are dyed a faint red and wisps of purplish cloud trail over them.

In summer the nights. Not only when the moon shines, but on dark nights too, as the fireflies flit to and fro, and even when it rains, how beautiful it is!

In autumn the evenings, when the glittering sun sinks close to the edge of the hills and the crows fly back to their nests in threes and fours and twos; more charming still is a file of wild geese, like specks in the distant sky. When the sun has set, one's heart is moved by the sound of the wind and the hum of the insects.

In winter the early mornings. It is beautiful indeed when snow has fallen during the night, but splendid too when the ground is white with frost; or even when there is no snow or frost, but it is simply very cold and the attendants hurry from room to room stirring up the fires and bringing charcoal, how well this fits the season's mood! But as noon approaches and the cold wears off, no one bothers to keep the braziers alight, and soon nothing remains but piles of white ashes.

DOROTHY WORDSWORTH
1771–1855

Typically overshadowed by her more famous brother, the Romantic poet William (1770–1850), Dorothy Wordsworth has come to be recognized as a skilful and absorbing author in her own right. Born in Cumberland and raised, for a time, in Halifax, West Yorkshire, she is most closely associated with Grasmere, the Cumbrian village where she regularly kept the diaries which have ensured her literary legacy. These posthumously published journals were unlikely to have been written for the public, lending them an informal tone which amplifies the striking effects of her alert descriptions, subtle lyricism and profound appreciation for nature. The extracts selected here are all drawn from the *Grasmere Journals* for 1802.

from *The Grasmere Journals*

Sunday, 7th February.—A fine clear frosty morning. The eaves drop with the heat of the sun all day long. The ground thinly covered with snow. The road black, rocks black. Before night the island was quite green. The sun had melted all the snow. [...]

Friday, 16th April (Good Friday).—When I undrew curtains in the morning, I was much affected by the beauty of the prospect, and the change. The sun shone, the wind had passed away, the hills looked cheerful, the river was very bright as it flowed into the lake. The church rises up behind a little knot of rocks, the steeple not so high as an ordinary three-story house. Trees in a row in the garden under the wall. The valley is at first broken by little woody knolls that make retiring places, fairy valleys in the vale, the river winds along under these hills, travelling, not in a bustle but not slowly, to the lake. We saw a fisherman in the flat meadow on the other side of the water. He came towards us, and threw his line over the two-arched bridge. It is a bridge of a heavy construction, almost bending inwards in the middle, but it is grey, and there is a look of ancientry in the architecture of it that pleased me.

As we go on the vale opens out more into one vale, with somewhat of a cradle bed. Cottages, with groups of trees, on the side of the hills. We passed a pair of twin children, two years old. Sate on the next bridge which we crossed—a single arch. We rested again upon the turf, and looked at the same bridge. We observed arches in the water, occasioned by the large stones sending it down in two streams. A sheep came plunging through the river, stumbled up the bank, and passed close to us. It had been frightened by an insignificant little dog on the other side. Its fleece dropped a glittering shower under its belly. Primroses by the road-side, pile wort that shone like stars of gold in the sun, violets, strawberries, retired and half-buried among the grass. When we came to the foot of Brothers Water, I left William sitting on the bridge, and went along the path on the right side of the lake through the wood. I was delighted with what I saw. The water under the boughs of the bare old trees, the simplicity of the mountains, and the exquisite beauty of the path. There was one grey cottage. I repeated *The Glow-worm*, as I walked along. I hung over the gate, and thought I could have stayed for ever. When I returned, I found William writing a poem descriptive of the sights and sounds we saw and heard. There was the gentle flowing of the

stream, the glittering, lively lake, green fields without a living creature to be seen on them; behind us,
a flat pasture with forty-two cattle feeding; to our
left, the road leading to the hamlet. No smoke
there, the sun shone on the bare roofs. The people
were at work ploughing, harrowing, and sowing; . . .
a dog barking now and then, cocks crowing, birds
twittering, the snow in patches at the top of the
highest hills, yellow palms, purple and green twigs
on the birches, ashes with their glittering stems
quite bare. The hawthorn a bright green, with black
stems under the oak. The moss of the oak glossy.
We went on. Passed two sisters at work (they first
passed us), one with two pitchforks in her hand, the
other had a spade. We had come to talk with them.
They laughed long after we were gone, perhaps half
in wantonness, half boldness. William finished his
poem.* Before we got to the foot of Kirkstone,
there were hundreds of cattle in the vale. There we
ate our dinner. The walk up Kirkstone was very
interesting. The becks among the rocks were all
alive. William showed me the little mossy streamlet
which he had before loved when he saw its bright
green track in the snow. The view above Ambleside
very beautiful. There we sate and looked down on

* See "The Cock is crowing," etc., vol. ii. p. 293.—ED.

the green vale. We watched the crows at a little distance from us become white as silver as they flew in the sunshine, and when they went still further, they looked like shapes of water passing over the green fields. The whitening of Ambleside church is a great deduction from the beauty of it, seen from this point. We called at the Luffs, the Roddingtons there. Did not go in, and went round by the fields. I pulled off my stockings, intending to wade the beck, but I was obliged to put them on, and we climbed over the wall at the bridge. The post passed us. No letters. Rydale Lake was in its own evening brightness: the Island, and Points distinct. Jane Ashburner came up to us when we were sitting upon the wall . . . The garden looked pretty in the half-moonlight, half-daylight, as we went up the vale . . .

[...]

Saturday, 19th.—The swallows were very busy under my window this morning . . . Coleridge, when he was last here, told us that for many years, there being no Quaker meeting at Keswick, a single old Quaker woman used to go regularly alone every Sunday to attend the meeting-house, and there used to sit and perform her worship alone, in that beautiful place among those fir trees, in that spacious vale, under the great mountain Skiddaw!!! . . . On Thursday morning Miss Hudson of Workington called. She said, ". . . I sow flowers in the parks several miles from home, and my mother and I visit them, and watch them how they grow." This may show that botanists may be often deceived when they find rare flowers growing far from houses. This was a very ordinary young woman, such as in any town in the North of England one may find a score. I sate up a while after William. He then called me down to him. (I was writing to Mary H.) I read Churchill's *Rosciad*. Returned again to my writing, and did not go to bed till he called to me. The shutters were closed, but I heard the birds singing. There was our own thrush, shouting with an impatient shout; so it sounded to me. The morning was still, the twittering of the little birds was very gloomy. The owls had hooted a quarter of an hour before, now the cocks were crowing, it was near daylight, I put out my candle, and went to bed . . .

[...]

24th December.—Christmas Eve. William is now sitting by me, at half-past ten o'clock. I have been . . . repeating some of his sonnets to him, listening to his own repeating, reading some of

Milton's, and the *Allegro* and *Penseroso*. It is a quick, keen frost . . . Coleridge came this morning with Wedgwood. We all turned out . . . one by one, to meet him. He looked well. We had to tell him of the birth of his little girl, born yesterday morning at six o'clock. William went with them to Wytheburn in the chaise, and M. and I met W. on the Raise. It was not an unpleasant morning . . . The sun shone now and then, and there was no wind, but all things looked cheerless and distinct; no meltings of sky into mountains, the mountains like stone work wrought up with huge hammers. Last Sunday was as mild a day as I ever remember . . . Mary and I went round the lakes. There were flowers of various kinds—the topmost bell of a foxglove, geraniums, daisies, a buttercup in the water (but this I saw two or three days before), small yellow flowers (I do not know their name) in the turf. A large bunch of strawberry blossoms . . . It is Christmas Day, Saturday, 25th December 1802. I am thirty-one years of age. It is a dull, frosty day.

SUSAN FENIMORE COOPER
1813–1894

Born in Scarsdale, New York, Susan Fenimore
Cooper was a novelist, essayist and amateur naturalist. During a long life, she also served as
amanuensis and literary executor for her father,
James Fenimore Cooper (1789–1851), bestselling
author of *The Last of the Mohicans* (1826). Her own
bestseller, *Rural Hours* (1850), was one of the first
pieces of nature writing published in the United
States and the first written by a woman. Darwin
praised it and Thoreau knew it – indeed, scholars
are still debating how much of *Walden* (1854)
converses with Cooper's 1850 work. An early cam-
paigner for the preservation of forests, she was one
of the first writers in the US to warn against the
overexploitation of natural resources. In these
extracts from *Rural Hours*, her lifelong love for
nature shines through her bright lucid style.

from *Rural Hours*

Friday, June 1st.—Beautiful day. Pleasant walk. The whole country is green at this moment, more so than at any other period of the year. The earth is completely decked in delicate verdure of varied shades: the fruit-trees have dropped their blossoms, and the orchards and gardens are green; the forest has just put on its fresh foliage, the meadows are yet uncolored by the flowers, and the young grain-fields look grassy still. This fresh green hue of the country is very charming, and with us it is very fugitive, soon passing away into the warmer coloring of midsummer.

The cedar-birds have been very troublesome among the fruit blossoms, and they are still haunting the gardens. As they always move in flocks, except for a very short period when busy with their young, they leave their mark on every tree they attack, whether in fruit or flower. We saw them last week scattering the petals in showers, to get at the heart of the blossom, which, of course, destroys the young fruit. They are very much their own enemies in this way, for no birds are greater fruit-eaters than themselves; they are even voracious feeders when they find a berry to their taste, actually destroying themselves, at times, by the numbers they swallow.

There are two closely-allied varieties of this bird, very similar in general appearance and character, one coming from the extreme north, while the other is found within the tropics. Both, however, meet on common ground in the temperate regions of our own country. The larger sort—the Bohemian wax-wing—is well known in Europe, though so irregular in its flights, that in former times its visits were looked upon by superstitious people as the forerunner of some public calamity. Until lately, this bird was supposed to be unknown on the Western continent; but closer observation has shown that it is found here, within our own State, where it is said to be increasing. It bears a strong general resemblance to the cedar-bird, though decidedly larger, and differently marked in some points. It is supposed to breed very far north in arctic countries. Both birds are crested, and both have a singular appendage to their wings, little red, wax-like, tips at the extremity of their secondary wing-feathers. These vary in number, and are not found on all individuals, but they are quite peculiar to themselves. The habits of the two varieties are, in many respects, similar: they are both berry-eaters, very gregarious in their habits, and particularly affectionate in their dispositions toward one another; they crowd as near together as possible, half a dozen often sitting side by side on the same branch, caressing one another, and even feeding one another out of pure friendliness. They have been called chatterers in the Old World, but in fact they are very silent birds, though fussy and active, which perhaps made people fancy they were chatty creatures also.

The Bohemian wax-wing is rather rare, even in Europe; and yet it is believed that a small flock were in our own neighborhood this spring. On two different occasions we remarked what seemed very large cedar-birds *without* the white line about the eye, and *with* a white stripe on the wings; but they were in a thicket both times, and not being at liberty to stay and watch them, it would not do to assert positively that these were the Bohemian wax-wing. Learned ornithologists, with a bird in the hand, have sometimes made great mistakes on such matters, and, of course, unlearned people should be very modest in expressing an opinion, especially where, instead of one bird in the hand, they can only point to two in a bush. As for the cedar-birds, everybody knows them; they are common enough throughout the country, and are also abundant in Mexico. They are sold in the markets of our large towns, in the autumn and spring, for two or three cents a piece.

Saturday, 2d.—Cloudy morning, followed by a charming afternoon. Long walk. Took a by-road which led us over the hills to a wild spot, where, in a distance of two or three miles, there is only one inhabited house, and that stands on the border of a gloomy swamp, from which the wood has been cut away, while two or three deserted log-cabins along the road only make things look more desolate. We enjoyed the walk all the more, however, for its wild, rude character, so different from our everyday rambles. Passed several beautiful springs in the borders of the unfenced woods, and saw several interesting birds. A handsome Clape, or golden-winged woodpecker, a pretty wood-pewce, and a very delicate little black-poll warbler, this last rare, and entirely confined to the forest; it was hopping very leisurely among the flowery branches of a wild cherry, and we had an excellent opportunity of observing it, for on that wild spot it was not on the look-out for human enemies, and we approached, unobserved, placing ourselves behind a bush. These three birds are all peculiar to our part of the world.

The rude fences about several fields in these new lands were prettily bordered with the Canadian violet, white and lilac; the chinks and hollows of several old stumps were also well garnished with these flowers; one does not often see so many together.

Upon one of these violets we found a handsome colored spider, one of the kind that live on flowers and take their color from them; but this was unusually large. Its body was of the size of a well-grown pea, and of a bright lemon color; its legs were also yellow, and altogether it was one of the most showy colored spiders we have seen in a long time. Scarlet, or red ones still larger, are found, however, near New York. But, in their gayest aspect, these creatures are repulsive. It gives one a chilling idea of the gloomy solitude of a prison, when we remember that spiders have actually been petted by men shut out from better companionship. They are a very common insect with us, and on that account more annoying than any other that is found here. Some of them, with great black bodies, are of a formidable size. These haunt cellars, and barns, and churches, and appear occasionally in inhabited rooms. There is a black spider of this kind, with a body said to be an inch long, and legs double that length, found in the Palace of Hampton Court, in England, which, it will be remembered, belonged to Cardinal Wolsey, and these great creatures are called "Cardinals" there, being considered by some people as peculiar to that building. A huge spider, by-the-bye, with her intricate web and snares, would form no bad emblem of a courtier and diplomatist, of the stamp of Cardinal Wolsey. He certainly took "hold with his hands, in kings' palaces," and did his share of mischief there.

Few people like spiders. No doubt these insects must have their merits and their uses, since none of God's creatures are made in vain; all living things are endowed with instincts more or less admirable; but the spider's plotting, creeping ways, and a sort of wicked expression about him, lead one to dislike him as a near neighbor. In a battle between a spider and a fly, one always sides with the fly, and yet of the two, the last is certainly the most troublesome insect to man. But the fly is frank and free in all his doings; he seeks his food openly, and he pursues his pastimes openly; suspicions of others or covert designs against them are quite unknown to him, and there is something almost confiding in the way in which he sails around you, when a single stroke of your hand might destroy him. The spider, on the contrary, lives by snares and plots; he is at the same time very designing and very suspicious, both cowardly and fierce; he always moves stealthily, as though among enemies, retreating before the least appearance of danger, solitary and morose, holding no communion with his fellows. His whole appearance corresponds with this character, and it is not surprising, therefore, that while the fly is more mischievous to us than the spider, we yet look upon the first with more favor than the last; for it is a natural impulse of the human heart to prefer that which is open and confiding to that which is wily and suspicious, even in the brute creation. The cunning and designing man himself will, at times, find a feeling of respect and regard for the guileless and generous stealing over him, his heart, as it were, giving the lie to his life.

Some two or three centuries since, when people came to this continent from the Old World in search of gold, oddly enough, it was considered a good sign of success when they met with spiders! It would be difficult to say why they cherished this fancy; but according to that old worthy, Hakluyt, when Martin Frobisher and his party landed on Cumberland Island, in quest of gold, their expectations were much increased by finding there numbers of spiders, "which, as many affirm, are signes of great store of gold."

They fancied that springs also were abundant near minerals, so that we may, in this county, cherish great hopes of a mine—if we choose.

WALT WHITMAN
1819–1892

Born to a down-on-their-luck family in Hunting-don, Long Island, Whitman spent much of his life in Brooklyn, New York. Forced to seek work from the age of eleven, he was employed in various capacities, at first in printing and journalism, then as a government clerk, and, later, as a nurse during the Civil War. His real labour, though, was *Leaves of Grass* (1855). Privately printed at the poet's expense, Whitman went on revising it until his death in 1892. Marked by King James cadences and an adoration of all that is natural and all that is human, *Leaves of Grass* was initially censured for its overtly sexual themes. Today it is recognized as an authentic literary classic. Alongside his poetry, Whitman kept extensive diaries, gathered in *Specimen Days and Collect* (1882). In these poignant prose fragments, he writes with sensitivity and wonder about encounters with birds and insects, languid evenings under a willow tree and subtle changes in the weather, fashioning gorgeous moving vistas of nature and experience.

from *Specimen Days and Collect*

NEW THEMES ENTERED UPON.

1876, '77. [...] Seated on logs or stumps there, or resting on rails, nearly all the following memoranda have been jotted down. Wherever I go, indeed, winter or summer, city or country, alone at home or traveling, I must take notes—(the ruling passion strong in age and disablement, and even the approach of—but I must not say it yet.) Then underneath the following excerpta—crossing the *t*'s and dotting the *i*'s of certain moderate movements of late years—I am fain to fancy the foundations of quite a lesson learn'd. After you have exhausted what there is in business, politics, conviviality, love, and so on—have found that none of these finally satisfy, or permanently wear—what remains? Nature remains; to bring out from their torpid recesses, the affinities of a man or woman with the open air, the trees, fields, the changes of seasons— the sun by day and the stars of heaven by night. [...]

Whether the rains, the heat and cold, and what underlies them all, are affected with what affects man in masses, and follow his play of passionate action, strain'd stronger than usual, and on a larger scale than usual—whether this, or no, it is certain that there is now, and has been for twenty months or more, on this American continent north, many a remarkable, many an unprecedented expression of the subtle world of air above us and around us. There, since this war, and the wide and deep national agitation, strange analogies, different combinations, a different sunlight, or absence of it; different products even out of the ground. After every great battle, a great storm. Even civic events the same. On Saturday last, a forenoon like whirling demons, dark, with slanting rain, full of rage; and then the afternoon, so calm, so bathed with flooding splendor from heaven's most excellent sun, with atmosphere of sweetness; so clear, it show'd the stars, long, long before they were due. As the President came out on the capitol portico, a curious little white cloud, the only one in that part of the sky, appear'd like a hovering bird, right over him.

Indeed, the heavens, the elements, all the meteorological influences, have run riot for weeks past. Such caprices, abruptest alternation of frowns and beauty, I never knew. It is a common remark that (as last summer was different in its spells of intense heat from any preceding it,) the winter just completed has been without parallel. It has remain'd so down to the hour I am writing. Much of the daytime of the past month was sulky, with leaden heaviness, fog, interstices of bitter cold, and some insane storms. But there have been samples of another description. Nor earth nor sky ever knew spectacles of superber beauty than some of the nights lately here. The western star, Venus, in the earlier hours of evening, has never been so large, so clear; it seems as if it told something, as if it held rapport indulgent with humanity, with us Americans. Five or six nights since, it hung close by the moon, then a little past its first quarter. The star was wonderful, the moon like a young mother. The sky, dark blue, the transparent night, the planets, the moderate west wind, the elastic temperature, the miracle of that great star, and the young and swelling moon swimming in the west, suffused the soul. Then I heard, slow and clear, the deliberate notes of a bugle come up out of the silence, sounding so good through the night's mystery, no hurry,

but firm and faithful, floating along, rising, falling
leisurely, with here and there a long-drawn note;
the bugle, well play'd, sounding tattoo, in one of
the army hospitals near here, where the wounded
(some of them personally so dear to me,) are lying
in their cots, and many a sick boy come down to
the war from Illinois, Michigan, Wisconsin, Iowa,
and the rest.

[...]

SPRING OVERTURES—RECREATIONS.

Feb. 10.—The first chirping, almost singing, of a
bird to-day. Then I noticed a couple of honey-bees
spirting and humming about the open window in
the sun.

Feb. 11.—In the soft rose and pale gold of the
declining light, this beautiful evening, I heard the
first hum and preparation of awakening spring—
very faint—whether in the earth or roots, or starting
of insects, I know not—but it was audible, as I
lean'd on a rail (I am down in my country quarters
awhile,) and look'd long at the western horizon.
Turning to the east, Sirius, as the shadows deepen'd,
came forth in dazzling splendor. And great Orion;
and a little to the north-east the big Dipper, standing on end.

Feb. 20.—A solitary and pleasant sundown hour at the pond, exercising arms, chest, my whole body, by a tough oak sapling thick as my wrist, twelve feet high—pulling and pushing, inspiring the good air. After I wrestle with the tree awhile, I can feel its young sap and virtue welling up out of the ground and tingling through me from crown to toe, like health's wine. Then for addition and variety I launch forth in my vocalism; shout declamatory pieces, sentiments, sorrow, anger, &c., from the stock poets or plays—or inflate my lungs and sing the wild tunes and refrains I heard of the blacks down south, or patriotic songs I learn'd in the army. I make the echoes ring, I tell you! As the twilight fell, in a pause of these ebullitions, an owl somewhere the other side of the creek sounded *too-oo-oo-oo-oo*, soft and pensive (and I fancied a little sarcastic) repeated four or five times. Either to applaud the negro songs—or perhaps an ironical comment on the sorrow, anger, or style of the stock poets.

[...]

THE COMMON EARTH, THE SOIL.
The soil, too—let others pen-and-ink the sea, the air, (as I sometimes try)—but now I feel to choose the common soil for theme—naught else. The brown soil here, (just between winter-close and

165

opening spring and vegetation)—the rain-shower at night, and the fresh smell next morning—the red worms wriggling out of the ground—the dead leaves, the incipient grass, and the latent life underneath—the effort to start something—already in shelter'd spots some little flowers—the distant emerald show of winter wheat and the rye-fields— the yet naked trees, with clear interstices, giving prospects hidden in summer—the tough fallow and the plow-team, and the stout boy whistling to his horses for encouragement—and there the dark fat earth in long slanting stripes upturn'd.

BIRDS AND BIRDS AND BIRDS.

A little later—bright weather.—An unusual melodiousness, these days, (last of April and first of May) from the blackbirds; indeed all sorts of birds, darting, whistling, hopping or perch'd on trees. Never before have I seen, heard, or been in the midst of, and got so flooded and saturated with them and their performances, as this current month. Such oceans, such successions of them. Let me make a list of those I find here:

Black birds (plenty,)
Ring doves,
Owls,
Woodpeckers,

King-birds,
Crows (plenty,)
Wrens,
Kingfishers,
Quails,
Turkey-buzzards,
Hen-hawks,
Yellow birds,
Thrushes,
Reed birds,
Meadow-larks (plenty,)
Cat-birds (plenty,)
Cuckoos,
Pond snipes (plenty,)
Cheewinks,
Quawks,
Ground robins,
Ravens,
Gray snipes,
Eagles,
High-holes,
Herons,
Tits,
Woodpigeons.

Early came the
Blue birds,

Killdeer,
Plover,
Robin,
Woodcock,
Meadow lark,
White-bellied swallow,
Sandpiper,
Wilson's thrush.
Flicker.

[...]

MATURE SUMMER DAYS AND NIGHTS.

Aug. 4.—Forenoon—as I sit under the willow shade, (have retreated down in the country again,) a little bird is leisurely dousing and flirting himself amid the brook almost within reach of me. He evidently fears me not—takes me for some concomitant of the neighboring earthy banks, free bushery and wild weeds. *6 p. m.*—The last three days have been perfect ones for the season, (four nights ago copious rains, with vehement thunder and lightning.) I write this sitting by the creek watching my two kingfishers at their sundown sport. The strong, beautiful, joyous creatures! Their wings glisten in the slanted sunbeams as they circle and circle around, occasionally dipping and dashing the water, and making long stretches up and down the creek. Wherever I go over fields, through lanes, in by-places, blooms the white-flowering wild-carrot, its delicate pat of snow-flakes crowning its slender stem, gracefully oscillating in the breeze.

[...]

SWALLOWS ON THE RIVER.

Sept. 3.—Cloudy and wet, and wind due east; air without palpable fog, but very heavy with moisture—welcome for a change. Forenoon, crossing the Delaware, I noticed unusual numbers of swallows in flight, circling, darting, graceful beyond description, close to the water. Thick, around the bows of the ferry-boat as she lay tied in her slip, they flew; and as we went out I watch'd beyond the pier-heads, and across the broad stream, their swift-winding loop-ribands of motion, down close to it, cutting and intersecting. Though I had seen swallows all my life, seem'd as though I never before realized their peculiar beauty and character in the landscape. (Some time ago, for an hour, in a huge old country barn, watching these birds flying, recall'd the 22d book of the Odyssey, where Ulysses slays the suitors, bringing things to *eclaircissement*, and Minerva, swallow-bodied, darts up through the spaces of the hall, sits high on a beam, looks complacently on the show of slaughter, and feels in her element, exulting, joyous.)

[...]

PRAIRIE ANALOGIES—THE TREE QUESTION.

The word Prairie is French, and means literally meadow. The cosmical analogies of our North American plains are the Steppes of Asia, the Pampas and Llanos of South America, and perhaps the Saharas of Africa. Some think the plains have been originally lake-beds; others attribute the absence of forests to the fires that almost annually sweep over them—(the cause, in vulgar estimation, of Indian summer.) The tree question will soon become a grave one. Although the Atlantic slope, the Rocky mountain region, and the southern portion of the Mississippi valley, are well wooded, there are here stretches of hundreds and thousands of miles where either not a tree grows, or often useless destruction has prevail'd; and the matter of the cultivation and spread of forests may well be press'd upon thinkers who look to the coming generations of the prairie States.

[...]

A HINT OF WILD NATURE.

Feb. 13.—As I was crossing the Delaware to-day, saw a large flock of wild geese, right overhead, not very high up, ranged in V-shape, in relief against the noon clouds of light smoke-color. Had a capital though momentary view of them, and then of their course on and on southeast, till gradually fading— (my eyesight yet first rate for the open air and its distances, but I use glasses for reading.) Queer thoughts melted into me the two or three minutes, or less, seeing these creatures cleaving the sky—the spacious, airy realm—even the prevailing smoke-gray color everywhere, (no sun shining)—the waters below—the rapid flight of the birds, appearing just for a minute—flashing to me such a hint of the whole spread of Nature, with her eternal unsophisticated freshness, her never-visited recesses of sea, sky, shore—and then disappearing in the distance.

LOAFING IN THE WOODS.

March 8.—I write this down in the country again, but in a new spot, seated on a log in the woods, warm, sunny, midday. Have been loafing here deep among the trees, shafts of tall pines, oak, hickory, with a thick undergrowth of laurels and grapevines— the ground cover'd everywhere by debris, dead leaves, breakage, moss—everything solitary, ancient, grim. Paths (such as they are) leading hither and yon—(how made I know not, for nobody seems to come here, nor man nor cattle-kind.) Temperature today about 60, the wind through the pine-tops; I sit and listen to its hoarse sighing above (and to the *stillness*) long and long, varied by aimless rambles in the old roads and paths, and by exercise-pulls at the young saplings, to keep my joints from getting stiff. Blue-birds, robins, meadow-larks begin to appear.

Next day, 9th.—A snowstorm in the morning, and continuing most of the day. But I took a walk over two hours, the same woods and paths, amid the falling flakes. No wind, yet the musical low murmur through the pines, quite pronounced, curious, like waterfalls, now still'd, now pouring again. All the senses, sight, sound, smell, delicately gratified. Every snowflake lay where it fell on the evergreens, holly-trees, laurels, &c., the multitudinous leaves and branches piled, bulging-white, defined by edge-lines of emerald—the tall straight columns of the plentiful bronzetopt pines—a slight resinous odor blending with that of the snow. (For there is a scent to everything, even the snow, if you can only detect it—no two places, hardly any two hours, anywhere, exactly alike. How different the odor of noon from midnight, or winter from summer, or a windy spell from a still one.)

PRESERVATION

RALPH WALDO EMERSON
1803–1882

Prolific lecturer and master essayist, pioneering philosopher and staunch abolitionist, Ralph Waldo Emerson has inspired generations of artists and thinkers to pursue and foster individual liberty, to counter and critique all that is crushing in modern society, and to revere and study nature in all its forms. Born in Boston, he lived for much of his life in Concord, Massachusetts, where, in the 1840s, he rented out his cabin on Walden Pond to a young writer named Henry David Thoreau. Emerson's contemporaries viewed him as a wise man, the Sage of Concord, as he was sometimes known, and his spiritual wisdom and stunning rhetoric won him international fame. His essay 'Nature' (1836) launched his literary career and remains one of his best-known works. The foundational document of transcendentalist philosophy, Emerson's essay sees in nature the divine, and the key to understanding ourselves and our world.

from 'Nature'

INTRODUCTION

Our age is retrospective. It builds the sepulchres of the fathers. It writes biographies, histories, and criticism. The foregoing generations beheld God and nature face to face; we, through their eyes. Why should not we also enjoy an original relation to the universe? Why should not we have a poetry and philosophy of insight and not of tradition, and a religion by revelation to us, and not the history of theirs? Embosomed for a season in nature, whose floods of life stream around and through us, and invite us by the powers they supply, to action proportioned to nature, why should we grope among the dry bones of the past, or put the living generation into masquerade out of its faded wardrobe? The sun shines to-day also. There is more wool and flax in the fields. There are new lands, new men, new thoughts. Let us demand our own works and laws and worship.

Undoubtedly we have no questions to ask which are unanswerable. We must trust the perfection of the creation so far, as to believe that whatever curiosity the order of things has awakened in our minds, the order of things can satisfy. Every man's condition is a solution in hieroglyphic to those inquiries he would put. He acts it as life, before he apprehends it as truth. In like manner, nature is already, in its forms and tendencies, describing its own design. Let us interrogate the great apparition, that shines so peacefully around us. Let us inquire, to what end is nature?

All science has one aim, namely, to find a theory of nature. We have theories of races and of functions, but scarcely yet a remote approach to an idea of creation. We are now so far from the road to truth, that religious teachers dispute and hate each other, and speculative men are esteemed unsound and frivolous. But to a sound judgment, the most abstract truth is the most practical. Whenever a true theory appears, it will be its own evidence. Its test is, that it will explain all phenomena. Now many are thought not only unexplained but inexplicable; as language, sleep, madness, dreams, beasts, sex.

Philosophically considered, the universe is composed of Nature and the Soul. Strictly speaking, therefore, all that is separate from us, all which Philosophy distinguishes as the NOT ME, that is, both nature and art, all other men and my own body, must be ranked under this name, NATURE. In enumerating the values of nature and casting up their sum, I shall use the word in both senses;—in its common and in its philosophical import. In inquiries so general as our present one, the inaccuracy is not material; no confusion of thought will occur. *Nature*, in the common sense, refers to essences unchanged by man; space, the air, the river, the leaf. *Art* is applied to the mixture of his will with the same things, as in a house, a canal, a statue, a picture. But his operations taken together are so insignificant, a little chipping, baking, patching, and washing, that in an impression so grand as that of the world on the human mind, they do not vary the result.

CHAPTER I.

To go into solitude, a man needs to retire as much from his chamber as from society. I am not solitary whilst I read and write, though nobody is with me. But if a man would be alone, let him look at the stars. The rays that come from those heavenly worlds, will separate between him and what he touches. One might think the atmosphere was made transparent with this design, to give man, in the heavenly bodies, the perpetual presence of the sublime. Seen in the streets of cities, how great they are! If the stars should appear one night in a thousand years, how would men believe and adore;

and preserve for many generations the remembrance of the city of God which had been shown! But every night come out these envoys of beauty, and light the universe with their admonishing smile.

The stars awaken a certain reverence, because though always present, they are inaccessible; but all natural objects make a kindred impression, when the mind is open to their influence. Nature never wears a mean appearance. Neither does the wisest man extort her secret, and lose his curiosity by finding out all her perfection. Nature never became a toy to a wise spirit. The flowers, the animals, the mountains, reflected the wisdom of his best hour, as much as they had delighted the simplicity of his childhood.

When we speak of nature in this manner, we have a distinct but most poetical sense in the mind. We mean the integrity of impression made by manifold natural objects. It is this which distinguishes the stick of timber of the wood-cutter, from the tree of the poet. The charming landscape which I saw this morning, is indubitably made up of some twenty or thirty farms. Miller owns this field, Locke that, and Manning the woodland beyond. But none of them owns the landscape. There is a property in the horizon which no man has but he whose eye can integrate all the parts, that is, the poet. This is the best part of these men's farms, yet to this their warranty-deeds give no title.

To speak truly, few adult persons can see nature. Most persons do not see the sun. At least they have a very superficial seeing. The sun illuminates only the eye of the man, but shines into the eye and the heart of the child. The lover of nature is he whose inward and outward senses are still truly adjusted to each other; who has retained the spirit of infancy even into the era of manhood. His intercourse with heaven and earth, becomes part of his daily food. In the presence of nature, a wild delight runs through the man, in spite of real sorrows. Nature says,—he is my creature, and maugre all his impertinent griefs, he shall be glad with me. Not the sun or the summer alone, but every hour and season yields its tribute of delight; for every hour and change corresponds to and authorizes a different state of the mind, from breathless noon to grimmest midnight. Nature is a setting that fits equally well a comic or a mourning piece. In good health, the air is a cordial of incredible virtue. Crossing a bare common, in snow puddles, at twilight, under a clouded sky, without having in my thoughts any occurrence of special good fortune, I have enjoyed a perfect exhilaration. I am glad to the brink of fear. In the woods too, a man casts off his years, as the snake his slough, and at what period soever of life, is always a child. In the woods, is perpetual youth. Within these plantations of God, a decorum and sanctity reign, a perennial festival is dressed, and the guest sees not how he should tire of them in a thousand years. In the woods, we return to reason and faith. There I feel that nothing can befall me in life,—no disgrace, no calamity, (leaving me my eyes,) which nature cannot repair. Standing on the bare ground,—my head bathed by the blithe air, and uplifted into infinite space,—all mean egotism vanishes. I become a transparent eye-ball; I am nothing; I see all; the currents of the Universal Being circulate through me; I am part or particle of God. The name of the nearest friend sounds then foreign and accidental: to be brothers, to be acquaintances,—master or servant, is then a trifle and a disturbance. I am the lover of uncontained and immortal beauty. In the wilderness, I find something more dear and connate than in streets or villages. In the tranquil landscape, and especially in the distant line of the horizon, man beholds somewhat as beautiful as his own nature.

The greatest delight which the fields and woods minister, is the suggestion of an occult relation between man and the vegetable. I am not alone and unacknowledged. They nod to me, and I to them. The waving of the boughs in the storm, is new to me and old. It takes me by surprise, and yet is not unknown. Its effect is like that of a higher thought or a better emotion coming over me, when I deemed I was thinking justly or doing right.

Yet it is certain that the power to produce this delight, does not reside in nature, but in man, or in a harmony of both.

LUTHER STANDING BEAR
1868–1939

Luther Standing Bear's eventful life was animated by a constant battle: to preserve Lakota heritage and to influence government policy towards Native Americans. Raised as a hunter and warrior by his father, a Sicangu chief, Luther Standing Bear was sent at the age of eleven to a Pennsylvanian boarding school which sought the complete cultural assimilation of Native Americans. This divided upbringing gave him a unique outlook. It allowed him to speak persuasively to an American public ill-informed about the realities of Native American culture and the hardships his people faced. As an educator and activist, he played a key role in popularizing the image of the Native American in harmony with nature, and his books, such as *Land of the Spotted Eagle* (1933), broadened support for Native American rights. Luther Standing Bear's writings transmit the principles of stewardship and respect for nature which he saw vanishing from humanity, and serve as a powerful attack on those who would exploit and exhaust the natural world.

from *Land of the Spotted Eagle*

The Lakota was a true naturist—a lover of Nature. He loved the earth and all things of the earth, the attachment growing with age. The old people came literally to love the soil and they sat or reclined on the ground with a feeling of being close to a mothering power. It was good for the skin to touch the earth and the old people liked to remove their moccasins and walk with bare feet on the sacred earth. Their tipis were built upon the earth and their altars were made of earth. The birds that flew in the air came to rest upon the earth and it was the final abiding place of all things that lived and grew. The soil was soothing, strengthening, cleansing, and healing.

This is why the old Indian still sits upon the earth instead of propping himself up and away from its life-giving forces. For him, to sit or lie upon the ground is to be able to think more deeply and to feel more keenly; he can see more clearly into the mysteries of life and come closer in kinship to other lives about him.

The earth was full of sounds which the old-time Indian could hear, sometimes putting his ear to it so as to hear more clearly. The forefathers of the Lakotas had done this for long ages until there had come to them real understanding of earth ways. It was almost as if the man were still a part of the earth as he was in the beginning, according to the legend of the tribe. This beautiful story of the genesis of the Lakota people furnished the foundation for the love they bore for earth and all things of the earth. Wherever the Lakota went, he was with Mother Earth. No matter where he roamed by day or slept by night, he was safe with her. This thought comforted and sustained the Lakota and he was eternally filled with gratitude.

From Wakan Tanka there came a great unifying life force that flowed in and through all things—the flowers of the plains, blowing winds, rocks, trees, birds, animals—and was the same force that had been breathed into the first man. Thus all things were kindred and brought together by the same Great Mystery.

Kinship with all creatures of the earth, sky, and water was a real and active principle. For the animal and bird world there existed a brotherly feeling that kept the Lakota safe among them. And so close did some of the Lakotas come to their feathered and furred friends that in true brotherhood they spoke a common tongue.

The animal had rights—the right of man's protection, the right to live, the right to multiply, the right to freedom, and the right to man's indebtedness—and in recognition of these rights the Lakota never enslaved the animal, and spared all life that was not needed for food and clothing.

This concept of life and its relations was humanizing and gave to the Lakota an abiding love. It filled his being with the joy and mystery of living; it gave him reverence for all life; it made a place for all things in the scheme of existence with equal importance to all. The Lakota could despise no creature, for all were of one blood, made by the same hand, and filled with the essence of the Great Mystery. In spirit the Lakota was humble and meek. 'Blessed are the meek: for they shall inherit the earth,' was true for the Lakota, and from the earth he inherited secrets long since forgotten. His religion was sane, normal, and human.

Reflection upon life and its meaning, consideration of its wonders, and observation of the world of creatures, began with childhood. The earth, which was called *Maka*, and the sun, called *Anpetuwi*, represented two functions somewhat analogous to those of male and female. The earth brought forth life, but the warming, enticing rays of the sun coaxed it into being. The earth yielded, the sun engendered.

In talking to children, the old Lakota would

place a hand on the ground and explain: 'We sit in the lap of our Mother. From her we, and all other living things, come. We shall soon pass, but the place where we now rest will last forever.' So we, too, learned to sit or lie on the ground and become conscious of life about us in its multitude of forms. Sometimes we boys would sit motionless and watch the swallow, the tiny ants, or perhaps some small animal at its work and ponder on its industry and ingenuity; or we lay on our backs and looked long at the sky and when the stars came out made shapes from the various groups. The morning and evening star always attracted attention, and the Milky Way was a path which was traveled by the ghosts. The old people told us to heed *wa maka skan*, which were the 'moving things of earth.' This meant, of course, the animals that lived and moved about, and the stories they told of *wa maka skan* increased our interest and delight. The wolf, duck, eagle, hawk, spider, bear, and other creatures, had marvelous powers, and each one was useful and helpful to us. Then there were the warriors who lived in the sky and dashed about on their spirited horses during a thunder storm, their lances clashing with the thunder and glittering with the lightning. There was *wiwila*, the living spirit of the spring, and the stones that flew like a bird and talked like a man. Everything was possessed of personality, only differing with us in form. Knowledge was inherent in all things. The world was a library and its books were the stones, leaves, grass, brooks, and the birds and animals that shared, alike with us, the storms and blessings of earth. We learned to do what only the student of nature ever learns, and that was to feel beauty. We never railed at the storms, the furious winds, and the biting frosts and snows. To do so intensified human futility, so whatever came we adjusted ourselves, by more effort and energy if necessary, but without complaint. Even the lightning did us no harm, for whenever it came too close, mothers and grandmothers in every tipi put cedar leaves on the coals and their magic kept danger away. Bright days and dark days were both expressions of the Great Mystery, and the Indian reveled in being close to the Big Holy. His worship was unalloyed, free from the fears of civilization.

I have come to know that the white mind does not feel toward nature as does the Indian mind, and it is because, I believe, of the difference in childhood instruction. I have often noticed white boys gathered in a city bystreet or alley jostling and pushing one another in a foolish manner. They spend much time in this aimless fashion, their natural faculties neither seeing, hearing, nor feeling the varied life that surrounds them. There is about them no awareness, no acuteness, and it is this dullness that gives ugly mannerisms full play; it takes from them natural poise and stimulation. In contrast, Indian boys, who are naturally reared, are alert to their surroundings; their senses are not narrowed to observing only one another, and they cannot spend hours seeing nothing, hearing nothing, and thinking nothing in particular. Observation was certain in its rewards; interest, wonder, admiration grew, and the fact was appreciated that life was more than mere human manifestation; that it was expressed in a multitude of forms. This appreciation enriched Lakota existence. Life was vivid and pulsing; nothing was casual and commonplace. The Indian lived—lived in every sense of the word—from his first to his last breath.

The character of the Indian's emotion left little room in his heart for antagonism toward his fellow creatures, this attitude giving him what is sometimes referred to as 'the Indian point of view.' Every true student, every lover of nature has 'the Indian point of view,' but there are few such students, for few white men approach nature in the Indian manner. The Indian and the white man sense things differently because the white man has put distance between himself and nature; and assuming a lofty place in the scheme of order of things has lost for him both reverence and understanding. Consequently the white man finds Indian philosophy obscure—wrapped, as he says, in a maze of ideas and symbols which he does not understand. A writer friend, a white man whose knowledge of 'Injuns' is far more profound and sympathetic than the average, once said that he had been privileged, on two occasions, to see the contents of an Indian medicine-man's bag in which were bits of earth, feathers, stones, and various other articles of symbolic nature; that a 'collector' showed him one and laughed, but a great and world-famous archaeologist showed him the other with admiration and wonder. Many times the Indian is embarrassed and baffled by the white man's allusions to nature in such terms as crude, primitive, wild, rude, untamed, and savage. For the Lakota, mountains, lakes, rivers, springs, valleys, and woods were all finished beauty; winds, rain, snow, sunshine, day, night, and change of seasons brought interest; birds, insects, and animals filled the world with knowledge that defied the discernment of man.

But nothing the Great Mystery placed in the land of the Indian pleased the white man, and nothing escaped his transforming hand. Wherever forests have not been mowed down; wherever the animal is recessed in their quiet protection; wherever the earth is not bereft of four-footed life—that to him is an 'unbroken wilderness.' But since for the Lakota there was no wilderness; since nature was not dangerous but hospitable; not forbidding but friendly, Lakota philosophy was healthy—free from fear and dogmatism. And here I find the great distinction between the faith of the Indian and the white man. Indian faith sought the harmony of man with his surroundings; the other sought the dominance of surroundings. In sharing, in loving all and everything, one people naturally found a measure of the thing they sought; while, in fearing, the other found need of conquest. For one man the world was full of beauty; for the other it was a place of sin and ugliness to be endured until he went to another world, there to become a creature of wings, half-man and half-bird. Forever one man directed his Mystery to change the world He had made; forever this man pleaded with Him to chastise His wicked ones; and forever he implored his Wakan Tanka to send His light to earth. Small wonder this man could not understand the other.

But the old Lakota was wise. He knew that

man's heart, away from nature, becomes hard; he knew that lack of respect for growing, living things soon led to lack of respect for humans too. So he kept his youth close to its softening influence.

CELIA THAXTER
1835–1894

Celia Thaxter spent most of her life on the Isles of
Shoals, a group of islands and tidal ledges a few
miles off the coastal border of Maine and New
Hampshire. Celebrated in her lifetime for her pastoral poetry and lyrical stories about her stunning
marine surroundings, she is now best remembered
for an essay, 'A Memorable Murder' (1875), which
recounts the gruesome killing of two sisters on
Smuttynose Island, close to Thaxter's home. This
grisly true-crime tale was very much an exception
in her work. *An Island Garden* (1894), excerpted
here, hews closer to the mood of Thaxter's other
writing. It is an attentive, awestruck account of
domesticated nature, her own green garden on
Appledore Island. Originally published alongside
artworks by the American Impressionist Childe
Hassam (1859–1935), Thaxter's evocative prose
makes illustrative claims of its own, and carries a
contagious passion for small miracles such as
poppy seeds, cornflowers, dandelions and toads.

from *An Island Garden*

Of all the wonderful things in the wonderful universe of God, nothing seems to me more surprising than the planting of a seed in the blank earth and the result thereof. Take a Poppy seed, for instance: it lies in your palm, the merest atom of matter, hardly visible, a speck, a pin's point in bulk, but within it is imprisoned a spirit of beauty ineffable, which will break its bonds and emerge from the dark ground and blossom in a splendor so dazzling as to baffle all powers of description.

The Genie in the Arabian tale is not half so astonishing. In this tiny casket lie folded roots, stalks, leaves, buds, flowers, seed-vessels,—surpassing color and beautiful form, all that goes to make up a plant which is as gigantic in proportion to the bounds that confine it as the Oak is to the acorn. You may watch this marvel from beginning to end in a few weeks' time, and if you realize how great a marvel it is, you can but be lost in "wonder, love, and praise." All seeds are most interesting, whether winged like the Dandelion and Thistle, to fly on every breeze afar; or barbed to catch in the wool of cattle or the garments of men, to be borne away and spread in all directions over the land; or feathered like the little polished silvery shuttlecocks of the Cornflower, to whirl in the wind abroad and settle presently, point downward, into the hospitable ground; or oared like the Maple, to row out upon the viewless tides of the air. But if I were to pause on the threshold of the year to consider the miracles of seeds alone, I should never, I fear, reach my garden plot at all!

He who is born with a silver spoon in his mouth is generally considered a fortunate person, but his good fortune is small compared to that of the happy mortal who enters this world with a passion for flowers in his soul. I use the word advisedly, though it seems a weighty one for the subject, for I do not mean a light or shallow affection, or even an æsthetic admiration; no butterfly interest, but a real love which is worthy of the name, which is capable of the dignity of sacrifice, great enough to bear discomfort of body and disappointment of spirit, strong enough to fight a thousand enemies for the thing beloved, with power, with judgment, with endless patience, and to give with everything else a subtler stimulus which is more delicate and perhaps more necessary than all the rest.

Often I hear people say, "How do you make your plants flourish like this?" as they admire the little flower patch I cultivate in summer, or the window gardens that bloom for me in the winter;

"I can never make my plants blossom like this! What is your secret?" And I answer with one word, "Love." For that includes all,—the patience that endures continual trial, the constancy that makes perseverance possible, the power of foregoing ease of mind and body to minister to the necessities of the thing beloved, and the subtle bond of sympathy which is as important, if not more so, than all the rest. For though I cannot go so far as a witty friend of mine, who says that when he goes out to sit in the shade on his piazza, his Wistaria vine leans toward him and lays her head on his shoulder, I am fully and intensely aware that plants are conscious of love and respond to it as they do to nothing else. You may give them all they need of food and drink and make the conditions of their existence as favorable as possible, and they may grow and bloom, but there is a certain ineffable something that will be missing if you do not love them, a delicate glory too spiritual to be caught and put into words. The Norwegians have a pretty and significant word, "Opelske," which they use in speaking of the care of flowers. It means literally "loving up," or cherishing them into health and vigor.

Like the musician, the painter, the poet, and the rest, the true lover of flowers is born, not made.

And he is born to happiness in this vale of tears, to a certain amount of the purest joy that earth can give her children, joy that is tranquil, innocent, uplifting, unfailing. Given a little patch of ground, with time to take care of it, with tools to work it and seeds to plant in it, he has all he needs, and Nature with her dews and suns and showers and sweet airs gives him her aid. But he soon learns that it is not only liberty of which eternal vigilance is the price; the saying applies quite as truly to the culture of flowers, for the name of their enemies is legion, and they must be fought early and late, day and night, without cessation. The cutworm, the wire-worm, the pansy-worm, the thrip, the rose-beetle, the aphis, the mildew, and many more, but worst of all the loathsome slug, a slimy, shapeless creature that devours every fair and exquisite thing in the garden,—the flower lover must seek all these with unflagging energy, and if possible exterminate the whole. So only may he and his precious flowers purchase peace. Manifold are the means of destruction to be employed, for almost every pest requires a different poison. On a closet shelf which I keep especially for them are rows of tin pepper-boxes, each containing a deadly powder, all carefully labeled. For the thrip that eats out the leaves of the Rosebush till they are nothing but fibrous skeletons of woody lace, there is hellebore, to be shaken on the under side of all the leaves,—mark you, the *under* side, and think of the difficulties involved in the process of so treating hundreds of leaves! For the blue or gray mildew and the orange mildew another box holds powdered sulphur,—this is more easily applied, shaken over the tops of the bushes, but all the leaves must be reached, none neglected at your peril! Still another box contains yellow snuff for the green aphis, but he is almost impossible to manage,—let once his legions get a foothold, good-by to any hope for you! Lime, salt, paris green, cayenne pepper, kerosene emulsion, whale-oil soap, the list of weapons is long indeed, with which one must fight the garden's foes! And it must be done with such judgment, persistence, patience, accuracy, and watchful care! It seems to me the worst of all the plagues is the slug, the snail without a shell. He is beyond description repulsive, a mass of sooty, shapeless slime, and he devours everything. He seems to thrive on all the poisons known; salt and lime are the only things that have power upon him, at least the only things I have been able to find so far. But salt and lime must be used very carefully, or they destroy the plant as effectually as the slug would do. Every night, while the season is yet young, and the precious growths just beginning to make their way upward, feeling their strength, I go at sunset and heap along the edge of the flower beds air-slaked lime, or round certain most valuable plants a ring of the same,—the slug cannot cross this while it is fresh, but should it be left a day or two it loses its strength, it has no more power to burn, and the enemy may slide over it unharmed, leaving his track of slime. On many a solemn midnight have I stolen from my bed to visit my cherished treasures by the pale glimpses of the moon, that I might be quite sure the protecting rings were still strong enough to save them, for the slug eats by night, he is invisible by day unless it rains or the sky be overcast. He hides under every damp board or in any nook of shade, because the sun is death to him. I use salt for his destruction in the same way as the lime, but it is so dangerous for the plants, I am always afraid of it. Neither of these things must be left about them when they are watered lest the lime or salt sink into the earth in such quantities as to injure the tender roots. I have little cages of fine wire netting which I adjust over some plants, carefully heaping the earth about them to leave no loophole through which the enemy may crawl, and round some of the beds, which are inclosed in strips of wood, boxed, to hold the earth in place, long shallow troughs of wood are nailed and filled with salt to keep off the pests. Nothing that human ingenuity can suggest do I leave untried to save my beloved flowers! Every evening at sunset I pile lime and salt about my pets, and every morning remove it before I sprinkle them at sunrise. The salt dissolves of itself in the humid sea air and in the dew, so around those for whose safety I am most solicitous I lay rings of pasteboard on which to heap it, to be certain of doing the plants no harm. Judge, reader, whether all this requires strength, patience, perseverance, hope! It is hard work beyond a doubt, but I do not grudge it, for great is my reward. Before I knew what to do to save my garden from the slugs, I have stood at evening rejoicing over rows of fresh emerald leaves just springing in rich lines along the beds, and woke in the morning to find the whole space stripped of any sign of green, as blank as a board over which a carpenter's plane has passed.

In the thickest of my fight with the slugs some one said to me, "Everything living has its enemy; the enemy of the slug is the toad. Why don't you import toads?"

I snatched at the hope held out to me, and immediately wrote to a friend on the continent,

"In the name of the Prophet, Toads!" At once a force of only too willing boys was set about the work of catching every toad within reach, and one day in June a boat brought a box to me from the far-off express office. A piece of wire netting was nailed across the top, and upon the earth with which it was half filled, reposing among some dry and dusty green leaves, sat three dry and dusty toads, wearily gazing at nothing. Is this all, I thought, only three! Hardly worth sending so far. Poor creatures, they looked so arid and wilted, I took up the hose and turned upon them a gentle shower of fresh cool water, flooding the box. I was not prepared for the result! The dry, baked earth heaved tumultuously; up came dusky heads and shoulders and bright eyes by the dozen. A sudden concert of liquid sweet notes was poured out on the air from the whole rejoicing company. It was really beautiful to hear that musical ripple of delight. I surveyed them with eager interest as they sat singing and blinking together. "You are not handsome," I said, as I took a hammer and wrenched off the wire cover that shut them in, "but you will be lovely in my sight if you will help me to destroy mine enemy;" and with that I turned the box on its side and out they skipped into a perfect paradise of food and shade. All summer I came upon them in different parts of the garden, waxing fatter and fatter till they were as round as apples. In the autumn baby toads no larger than my thumb nail were found hopping merrily over the whole island. There were sixty in that first importation; next summer I received ninety more. But alas! small dogs discover them to death, and the rats prey upon them so that many perish in that way; yet I hope to keep enough to preserve my garden in spite of fate.

GEORGE ORWELL
1903–1950

Born in British India into what he himself described as a 'lower-upper-middle class' family, Eric Arthur Blair's uncompromising moral seriousness and disdain for spurious comforts led the Eton-educated Blair to invent George Orwell. Under this unassuming alias, Orwell published essays, fiction and reportage which won him worldwide recognition. Famous for his lucid prose, shrewd political analysis and devotion to social justice, he was variously a journalist, teacher and bookseller, an officer in the Imperial Police in Burma and a soldier in the Spanish Civil War, a tramp in London and a dishwasher in Paris, a contributor to radio propaganda during the Second World War and an indefatigable book reviewer. He is best remembered for his novels *Animal Farm* (1945) and *Nineteen Eighty-Four* (1949), literary classics widely read for their anti-totalitarian stance, and for his gimlet-eyed essays such as 'Politics and the English Language' (1946). His article 'Some Thoughts on the Common Toad' (1946), reproduced here, starts as a deliberately trivial account of springtime in England and finishes with a powerful political message.

'Some Thoughts on the Common Toad'

Before the swallow, before the daffodil, and not much later than the snowdrop, the common toad salutes the coming of spring after his own fashion, which is to emerge from a hole in the ground, where he has lain buried since the previous autumn, and crawl as rapidly as possible towards the nearest suitable patch of water. Something – some kind of shudder in the earth, or perhaps merely a rise of few degrees in the temperature – has told him that it is time to wake up: though a few toads appear to sleep the clock round and miss out a year from time to time – at any rate, I have more than once dug them up, alive and apparently well, in the middle of summer.

At this period, after his long fast, the toad has a very spiritual look, like a strict Anglo-Catholic towards the end of Lent. His movements are languid but purposeful, his body is shrunken, and by contrast his eyes look abnormally large. This allows one to notice, what one might not at another time, that a toad has about the most beautiful eye of any living creature. It is like gold, or more exactly it is like the golden-coloured semi-precious stone which one sometimes sees in signet-rings, and which I think is called a chrysoberyl.

For a few days after getting into the water the toad concentrates on building up his strength by eating small insects. Presently he has swollen to his normal size again, and then he goes through a phase of intense sexiness. All he knows, at least if he is a male toad, is that he wants to get his arms round something, and if you offer him a stick, or even your finger, he will cling to it with surprising strength and take a long time to discover that it is not a female toad. Frequently one comes upon shapeless masses of ten or twenty toads rolling over and over in the water, one clinging to another without distinction of sex. By degrees, however, they sort themselves out into couples, with the male duly sitting on the female's back. You can now distinguish males from females, because the male is smaller, darker and sits on top, with his arms tightly clasped round the female's neck. After a day or two the spawn is laid in long strings which wind themselves in and out of the reeds and soon become invisible. A few more weeks, and the water is alive with masses of tiny tadpoles which rapidly grow larger, sprout hind-legs, then forelegs, then shed their tails: and finally, about the middle of the summer, the new generation of toads, smaller than one's thumb-nail but perfect in every particular, crawl out of the water to begin the game anew.

I mention the spawning of the toads because it is one of the phenomena of spring which most deeply appeal to me, and because the toad, unlike the skylark and the primrose, has never had much of a boost from poets. But I am aware that many people do not like reptiles or amphibians, and I am not suggesting that in order to enjoy the spring you have to take an interest in toads. There are also the crocus, the missel-thrush, the cuckoo, the blackthorn, etc. The point is that the pleasures of spring are available to everybody, and cost nothing. Even in the most sordid street the coming of spring will register itself by some sign or other, if it is only a brighter blue between the chimney pots or the vivid green of an elder sprouting on a blitzed site. Indeed it is remarkable how Nature goes on existing unofficially, as it were, in the very heart of London. I have seen a kestrel flying over the Deptford gasworks, and I have heard a first-rate performance by a blackbird in the Euston Road. There must be some hundreds of thousands, if not millions, of birds living inside the four-mile radius, and it is rather a pleasing thought that none of them pays a halfpenny of rent.

As for spring, not even the narrow and gloomy streets round the Bank of England are quite able to exclude it. It comes seeping in everywhere, like one of those new poison gases which pass through all filters. The spring is commonly referred to as 'a miracle', and during the past five or six years this worn-out figure of speech has taken on a new lease of life. After the sort of winters we have had to endure recently, the spring does seem miraculous, because it has become gradually harder and harder to believe that it is actually going to happen. Every February since 1940 I have found myself thinking that this time winter is going to be permanent. But Persephone, like the toads, always rises from the dead at about the same moment. Suddenly, towards the end of March, the miracle happens and the decaying slum in which I live is transfigured. Down in the square the sooty privets have turned bright green, the leaves are thickening on the chestnut trees, the daffodils are out, the wallflowers are budding, the policeman's tunic looks positively a pleasant shade of blue, the fishmonger greets his customers with a smile, and even the sparrows are quite a different colour, having felt the balminess of the air and nerved themselves to take a bath, their first since last September.

Is it wicked to take a pleasure in spring and other seasonal changes? To put it more precisely, is it politically reprehensible, while we are all groaning, or at any rate ought to be groaning, under the shackles of the capitalist system, to point out that life is frequently more worth living because of a blackbird's song, a yellow elm tree in October, or some other natural phenomenon which does not cost money and does not have what the editors of left-wing newspapers call a class angle? There is no doubt that many people think so. I know by experience that a favourable reference to 'Nature' in one of my articles is liable to bring me abusive letters, and though the keyword in these letters is usually 'sentimental', two ideas seem to be mixed up in them. One is that any pleasure in the actual process of life encourages a sort of political quiet-ism. People, so the thought runs, ought to be discontented, and it is our job to multiply our wants and not simply to increase our enjoyment of the things we have already. The other idea is that this is the age of machines and that to dislike the machine, or even to want to limit its domination, is backward-looking, reactionary and slightly ridiculous. This is often backed up by the state-ment that a love of Nature is a foible of urbanized people who have no notion what Nature is really like. Those who really have to deal with the soil, so it is argued, do not love the soil, and do not take the faintest interest in birds or flowers, except from a strictly utilitarian point of view. To love the country one must live in the town, merely taking an occasional week-end ramble at the warmer times of year.

This last idea is demonstrably false. Medieval literature, for instance, including the popular ballads, is full of an almost Georgian enthusiasm for Nature, and the art of agricultural peoples such as the Chinese and Japanese centres always round trees, birds, flowers, rivers, mountains. The other idea seems to me to be wrong in a subtler way. Certainly we ought to be discontented, we ought not simply to find out ways of making the best of a bad job, and yet if we kill all pleasure in the actual process of life, what sort of future are we preparing for ourselves? If a man cannot enjoy the return of spring, why should he be happy in a labour-saving Utopia? What will he do with the leisure that the machine will give him? I have always suspected that if our economic and political problems are ever really solved, life will become simpler instead of more complex, and that the sort of pleasure one gets from finding the first primrose will loom larger than the sort of pleasure one gets from eating an ice to the tune of a Wurlitzer. I think that by retaining one's childhood love of such things as trees, fishes, butterflies and – to return to my first instance – toads, one makes a peaceful and decent future a little more probable, and that by preaching the doctrine that nothing is to be admired except steel and concrete, one merely makes it a little surer that human beings will have no outlet for their surplus energy except in hatred and leader worship.

At any rate, spring is here, even in London N.1, and they can't stop you enjoying it. This is a satisfying reflection. How many a time have I stood watching the toads mating, or a pair of hares having a boxing match in the young corn, and thought of all the important persons who would stop me enjoying this if they could. But luckily they can't. So long as you are not actually ill, hungry, frightened or immured in a prison or a holiday camp, spring is still spring. The atom bombs are piling up in the factories, the police are prowling through the cities, the lies are streaming from the loudspeakers, but the earth is still going round the sun, and neither the dictators nor the bureaucrats, deeply as they disapprove of the process, are able to prevent it.

Permissions Acknowledgements

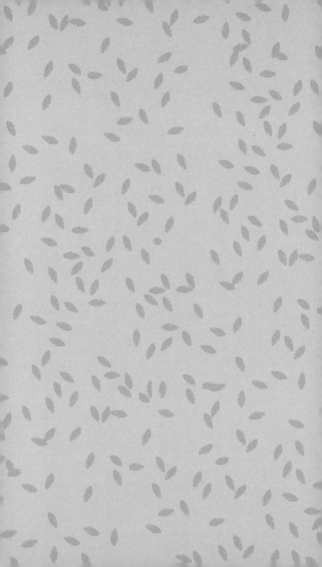